MAN OF VISION

Man of Vision

The Candid, Compelling Story of
Bob and Lorraine Pierce,
Founders of World Vision
and Samaritan's Purse

Marilee Pierce Dunker

Published in partnership with World Vision Press

Authentic Media
We welcome your comments and questions.
129 Mobilization Drive, Waynesboro, GA 30830 USA
authenticusa@stl.org
and 9 Holdom Avenue, Bletchley, Milton Keynes, Bucks, MK1 1QR, UK
www.authenticbooks.com

If you would like a copy of our current catalog, contact us at:
1-8MORE-BOOKS
ordersusa@stl.org

Man of Vision
ISBN: 1-932805-39-7 (book)
         1-932805-40-0 (audio cassette)
         1-932805-41-9 (audio CD)

Previously published under the titles:
         Days of Glory, Seasons of Night
         Man of Vision, Woman of Prayer

Published in partnership with World Vision
34834 Weyerhaeuser Way South, P.O. Box 9716
Federal Way, WA 98063 USA
www.worldvision.org

Cover design: Grey Matter Group
Interior design: John Veldboom
Editorial team: Karen James and Tom Richards

Printed in the United States of America

Dear Reader,

World Vision invites you to share your response to the message of this book by writing to World Vision Press at worldvisionpress@worldvision.org or by calling 800-777-7752.

For information about other World Vision Press publications, visit us at www.worldvision.org/worldvisionpress.

Contents

FOREWORD

Do not merely listen to the word. . . . Do what it says.
James 1:22

The most amazing thing about Bob and Lorraine Pierce was that they were ordinary people, but ordinary people with an extraordinary understanding of what it meant to be committed to Christ. Simply put, for them, faith in Christ was an all or nothing commitment. It meant "betting the farm" and holding back nothing; no easy believism or prosperity gospel, but a deep and costly journey of sacrifice and hardship.

Bob's now famous prayer captured this commitment in simple words: "*let my heart be broken by the things that break the heart of God.*" For Bob and Lorraine there was no compromise. If God's heart was broken by poverty, suffering, and brokenness, then they had to do everything in their power to bring hope, healing, and reconciliation to the least among us. You can see this same kind of sold out faith in David as he faced Goliath, Abraham as he took Isaac to Mount Moriah to sacrifice him, Noah as he built an ark in the midst of a desert, and in Paul who renounced all to bring the gospel to the gentiles. In this kind of faith, nothing is

1

held back, no price is too high to pay, the farm is bet, and the deed is signed over.

There is no comparison between this kind of faith and the more anemic form that offers a comfortable prosperity focused on meeting "my" needs and making "me" a better and happier "me." Authentic Christianity is a faith that reaches out to soothe and comfort the pain of others. It is a faith rooted in the heart of God and expressed in works. It is a faith of personal sacrifice and it comes with a cost.

Bob and Lorraine were not perfect people and this honest look at their lives does not gloss over their shortcomings or their struggles. Like David, Bob Pierce was a man with flaws and failings. He struggled all of his life with depression and emotional problems. He was estranged from his wife and children for many years and went to extremes in almost everything he did. And as you will see, the Pierce family paid a great price. Their service to God did not come without a heavy cost; true faith never does. But their legacy should inspire all of us "ordinary Christians." God is not looking for perfect people to do his work in the world. He is looking for willing people who will "bet the farm" on him.

In 1974, as a young man getting an MBA at the Wharton School of Business in Pennsylvania, I knelt down one day in my room and did just that. As an avowed agnostic and confirmed skeptic, my own commitment to Christ did not come easily. It came only after reading some fifty books and asking every question imaginable. But at that moment of decision, somehow I knew this much; that I was making an all or nothing commitment and that I would follow my Savior wherever he led me, whatever the cost.

Twenty-four years later, in the midst of a high profile corporate career, my phone would ring with the news that World Vision was seeking a new president. How could I refuse a call to serve my Lord in a ministry so close to his heart, demonstrating his love and compassion to the poorest of the poor? You see, the trail had already been blazed for me and the rocks and stones cleared to the side. I had only to follow in the footsteps of the giants that had preceded me. Those giants were Bob and Lorraine Pierce, and this is their story.

We're told in Scripture that if we have the faith of even a mustard seed we can command a mountain and hurl it into the sea. When I reflect back on the tiny seed of faith they planted in 1950, I marvel at what God has built on the sincere commitment of just two ordinary people. World Vision today touches 100 million of the world's poor in more than 100 countries with an annual budget approaching two billion dollars. Our 22,000 staff around the world are from every race, ethnicity, and denomination but they have two things in common; their hearts are broken by the things that break the heart of God, and they are determined to put their faith into action, whatever the cost. They've "bet the farm." You see, the hearts of Bob and Lorraine Pierce still beat strongly within World Vision.

> The kingdom of heaven is like a mustard seed, which a man took and planted in his field. Though it is the smallest of all your seeds, yet when it grows, it is the largest of garden plants and becomes a tree, so that the birds of the air come and perch in its branches. Matthew 13:31–32

Rich Stearns
President, World Vision US

INTRODUCTION

"Are you the daughter who wrote the book?"

The question took me by surprise. I was sitting at a banquet table with a group of pastors from the Philadelphia area who had gathered at World Vision's invitation to learn more about the AIDS pandemic, and we had only briefly introduced ourselves.

"Yes," I answered.

The pastor rose from his seat and walked over to my chair. "I read your book early in my ministry. It helped me to see the importance of prioritizing my marriage. My ministry and life were never the same. I just needed to say thank you," he said, giving me a hug.

I watched him walk back to his seat, feeling both humbled and amazed. In the twenty-five years since *Man of Vision* was first released I have had hundreds of similar encounters and received countless letters from those whose lives have been blessed in a significant way by my parents' story. Even after the book went out of print, it was kept alive through the Bible colleges and seminaries that duplicated it at their own expense. Now we have a new opportunity to share this incredible story of God's faithfulness with a new generation.

When I began researching this book I had no idea of the magnitude of my parents' story, nor of the ongoing impact it would have. Not one area of human experience is untouched—from the highest peaks of joy and accomplishment to the deepest pits of despair and defeat. It is a story filled with adventure, drama, and romance. But most of all it is a story of miracles . . . incredible miracles that remind us that we serve a God of the impossible and that embolden us to step out in our own journey of faith with renewed hope and confidence.

However, there is no point in writing about miracles if one is not willing to expose the battle so that the subsequent redemptive work of God can be fully appreciated. I wrote this book the only way I knew how, telling the story with the kind of straightforward honesty that it deserved. Consequently, anyone who reads this account must be prepared to be both emotionally and spiritually challenged, for this is the story of two very human people who were called of God, not to be perfect, but to be used to accomplish His will.

"Our lives were perfect examples of 1 Corinthians 1:27," my mother recently observed with the candor of her eighty plus years. "We were often weak and foolish, but God was *always* faithful!"

Undoubtedly there will be those who will ask if it was necessary or wise to be so honest.

You hold our answer in your hand. Rarely is anything accomplished for the kingdom of God without a very real spiritual battle proportionate to the magnitude of the work being done. God honored my parents faith by privileging them to give birth to two ministries (World Vision and Samaritan's Purse) that have reached around the world and literally transformed the lives of millions in the name of Jesus. Consequently the personal warfare they faced was unusually intense and vicious. To talk about the thrilling, positive things God did in my parents' lives without showing the satanic attacks and wilderness experiences they went through would be a disservice both to them and to the reader. It would also present a distorted picture of how God works, for nothing of any real value or lasting significance comes without a price.

This book is written as an expression of praise to our Lord Jesus Christ for his continuing work of grace and mercy in our lives as a family, and as a loving tribute to two people who were willing to pay the price.

1 UNCOMMON MAN, UNCOMMON WOMAN

"So many suffer so much while so few sacrifice so little." My father first spoke those words in 1951 in one of his first films, *New China Challenge*. Only three years before, he had traveled through China as an evangelist, seeing more than twenty thousand people receive Christ as their Savior. But within weeks of his return, China was swallowed whole by the governmental dragon of darkness called communism. Believers were systematically purged in an attempt to snuff out the flame of faith ignited during what many called the greatest spiritual revival in China's history.

Two years later, Daddy witnessed similar tragedy in Korea. Shaken by the naked, desperate pain and need of the people, he wrote in his Bible, "Let my heart be broken with the things that break the heart of God." Out of that brokenness of heart and his determination to do something about the suffering around him, World Vision was born. Today it is the largest Christian relief and development organization in the world.

But what does it cost to touch the world for Christ? What does it cost in terms of loneliness, personal tragedy, and tears? How do you put a price on the life of a child or the death of a marriage? How much of the price is the family expected to pay? And when all is said and done, *is it* worth the price?

On September 6, 1978, Robert Willard Pierce went to be with his Lord. Nearly one thousand people gathered to pay tribute to his memory. Almost everyone there had a story to tell of how Dr. Bob had been used by God to meet a desperate need, whether to raise $100,000 for a new hospital wing or to pray for a child dying of malnutrition. His work throughout the Orient—especially Korea and, later, Vietnam—is legendary to this day.

Bob Pierce specialized in the impossible. His whole life illustrated the saying, "They forgot to tell him it couldn't be done, so he did it."

Missionaries loved him because he truly understood their needs, both physical and emotional. He knew how important it was for a husband to have a few days away with his wife, or for missionary children to have a special Christmas. For these people, his efforts on their behalf sometimes meant the difference between giving up and going on.

To thousands of children orphaned by war or some other tragedy, to countless sick, crippled, and starving people, Bob Pierce came in the name of Jesus, offering both physical and spiritual health. My father often said, "You can't feed a starving man's spirit if you don't first feed his stomach."

My father had an unusual ability to "weep with those who weep," and he was driven relentlessly to do something about the intolerable pain and despair he saw.

But Bob Pierce was a man of flesh and blood, and some of his greatest strengths were related to his greatest weaknesses. His very need to minister to the multitudes often made it hard for him to recognize the desperate needs of those closest to him, or to allow himself the luxury of expressing his own needs.

Sitting at his memorial service, my heart was flooded with the painful realization that my father was really gone. My entire life had been punctuated by trips to the airport to kiss Daddy good-bye before he flew off to some distant land across the ocean. But this good-bye was different; the sense of loss was much deeper.

As one man after another stood to speak of the miracles God had worked through my father's life, I wondered how many people were aware of the miracles we as a family had experienced, as time and again the enemy had sought to destroy us. I looked at my mother, her face composed but pale with grief, and I wondered how many people knew anything of this woman who for forty years had participated in every aspect of Daddy's ministry through her undying love, her unshakable faith, and her continual prayers.

Mother's sentimental heart has always found it hard to throw things away. She has boxes full of her children's original poems, crayoned artwork, special cards, and little love notes. She also carefully preserved every letter Daddy wrote her through twenty-five years of travel and separation.

The first time I read these letters I was enthralled by the story they told. Here was the account of one of this generation's most phenomenal adventures in faith, recorded as it was happening by the man who was privileged to live it. In this day when the world and even much of the church takes a skeptical attitude toward God's wonder-working power, these letters testify to the fact that God is still the one through whom "all things are possible." Yet the letters were not written with posterity in mind; rather, they are tender declarations of love, intimate revelations of a man's heart to the one person in the world he could trust with his innermost thoughts and feelings.

Some people may have thought my parents were mismatched; Daddy was constantly on the go, and Mother seemed to be a homebody. But God brought Bob Pierce and Lorraine Johnson together, knowing that in them he had a unique and necessary combination—a man of great passion and courage, whose humanity might sometimes cause him to stumble but whose heart always desired the will of God, and a woman whose outward frailties were no indication of her inward strengths. This woman would have the courage to send her man to the ends of the earth and raise her children alone, because she trusted God to be her strength and provider.

This is the remarkable story of two ordinary people who believed that God could do extraordinary things in them and through them—a man of vision and a woman of prayer.

2 THE SCARLET THREAD

My parents' story doesn't begin with the day they met, or even with their birthdays.

My mother's father used to preach a sermon entitled "The Scarlet Thread." In it he described our spiritual heritage as a scarlet thread winding its way from one generation of believers to the next, starting from the foot of the cross upon which Jesus died. Both of my paternal grandparents loved the Lord and on my mother's side that scarlet thread can be traced back as far as my great-great-great-grandmother!

I hold in my hand four pieces of yellowing note paper that are precious beyond words. In flowing handwriting my mother's great-grandmother, Helen Cathrine Palmgren, wrote her testimony on these pages over a hundred years ago. Helen's mother was a Christian "whose consistent life and earnest prayers put a genuine desire in my young heart . . . to become a Christian." Helen received the Lord at fifteen but lived until the age of twenty-six without any assurance that her sins were forgiven. Then a traveling evangelist came to town, preaching "salvation full and free."

"Oh, my poor, stammering tongue cannot begin to express the flood of joy and peace that swept into my soul when I found that I was free," she wrote.

The scarlet thread wove its way from Helen down through her only child, Emma, to my grandfather, Floyd Ballington Johnson. Grandpa Johnson was not only an unshakable source of love and support to my mother, but he had an immeasurable influence on my father's life and ministry.

Papa, as we affectionately called him, grew up with a deep respect for God and authority. He went to church, read the Bible, and prayed to the God his mother knew so well. But it wasn't until he was twenty-three that a visiting evangelist confronted him with the need for more than a passing acquaintance with God. When the service was over, my grandfather waited in a long line to shake hands with this man whom God had used so powerfully. Paul Rader clasped Papa's hand warmly, sensing something special about this intense young man. In fact, after talking with Papa, Rader invited him to join his ministry if he ever felt God leading that way.

Papa was interested, but first he had to go home and try to explain to my grandmother this miracle of rebirth he had just experienced. Ethel Neimeyer Johnson came from a strong Methodist background, but had never come into a personal relationship with Jesus. Thus, the radical changes in her previously easygoing young husband were a bit disconcerting to her. But the love she and Papa shared was strong and deep, and Grammy did her best to adjust.

Into this home of strict religious doctrine and warm human relationships, my mother was born. Her memories of early childhood are full of sweet, simple pleasures like warm summer days picnicking beside the Des Plaines River and huge chocolate sodas at Walgreen's drug store.

Monday was always washday and also the day that Grammy would fill her largest kettle with homemade German sauerkraut and large meaty ribs, allowing the mixture to simmer the entire afternoon until the whole house was filled with the pungent odor and the meat separated in tender chunks from the bones. On Friday, Grammy would gather up the newspapers from underfoot to reveal her spotless kitchen floor. Then, with the determination of a true Swiss housewife, she would scrub every inch, covering the floor with fresh newspapers as soon as it was dry. As a small child, Mama always felt a flutter of surprise whenever she saw a bare floor without its proper covering of newspaper.

And so Mama's early years are rich in sweet memories, providing a foundation of love upon which she would someday build her own family.

When Mama was nine, my grandfather quit his job with Sunkist and joined Paul Rader's ministry. The Chicago Gospel Tabernacle was one of the most influential spiritual forces of its day. Rader's ministry was nationwide, and as one of his right-hand men, my grandfather's life was no longer his own. The demands of ministry were constant and ever increasing as Papa grew under Rader's discipleship and began developing his own ministry potential.

Both Papa and Grammy were active in the Tabernacle's music ministry. Papa had one of the country's first Christian radio programs—"The Sunshine Man"—which presented live gospel music over station WHT from the Wrigley Building in Chicago. Papa also began a powerful preaching ministry during this time, and after about four years he decided it was time to step out on his own.

Grammy had loved the excitement of being at the Tabernacle; but when Papa began traveling as an evangelist, she found herself an "evangelistic widow," a role she was unprepared to accept. Eventually my grandparents were separated, a fact that deeply wounded my mother and caused her to be estranged from my grandmother for many years.

In the spring of 1936, Papa was invited by a group of Nazarene churches to hold a series of evangelistic meetings in the Los Angeles area. Mama was a typical eighteen-year-old—pretty, perky, and caught up in her own world. At the time, she was informally engaged to Bill, a nice, responsible Christian boy with no unsettling plans to save the world or travel more than once a year. Going to California would mean leaving her friends, quitting her job, and most unbearable of all, saying good-bye to Bill for two whole months.

But Mama loved her father dearly, and she couldn't bear the thought of sending him on the long trip all alone. So she settled herself in Papa's new Buick for the long drive from Chicago to Los Angeles. Bemoaning her fate with every passing mile, she fervently prayed, "You know I love you, Lord. But don't ever ask me to marry a traveling evangelist!"

• • •

"Lorraine, you've just got to meet Bob Pierce. He's studying for the ministry at Pasadena Nazarene College, and he's darling!"

Mama just smiled at her new friend, Virginia Wallin, daughter of the pastor of the First Church of the Nazarene in Los Angeles. She was in love with Bill and not interested in other boys.

But one night when Papa Johnson was speaking at the Long Beach Church of the Nazarene, Mama was surprised to hear Pastor Williams call Bob Pierce to the platform to lead in prayer. She watched with interest as the slender, curly-haired young man worked his way to the front, took the steps to the platform two at a time, and presented himself with unusual assurance before the large crowd. *So this is the one Virginia keeps talking about,* Mama thought. Her heart began to beat a little faster as she studied his deep-set blue eyes and his warm, spontaneous smile.

Seated on the platform that night, Bob Pierce had a bird's-eye view of the audience. More than one person had told him he should meet Floyd Johnson's pretty daughter, and he found himself trying to pick her out of the crowd. His eyes returned several times to a lovely, fresh-faced girl with soft brown hair and gentle green eyes. Somehow he knew she was the girl he had been hearing about.

After the service, Mama made her way to the front of the auditorium, hoping to be introduced. But Daddy was praying with someone who had come forward to receive Jesus. And Papa was scheduled to do a radio program right after the service, so he needed to leave. With one last look, Mama was propelled out the door and rushed to the KPOX radio station across town.

During the radio broadcast, Mama's thoughts kept drifting back to the image of Bob Pierce weeping unashamedly as he knelt in prayer beside a new child of God. There was something about him that had touched her heart, even though they had never even met.

When the program was over, Pastor and Mrs. Williams invited them for hot fudge sundaes. Unable to shake her disappointment, Mama watched her ice cream melt while the others talked excitedly about the wonderful things God had done that night.

Suddenly the conversation stopped, and Mama looked up to see two young men standing hesitantly at the door, waving at Mrs. Williams. She excused herself, talked to them a minute, and then invited them to the table.

"Lorraine, I'd like you to meet Bob Pierce. Bob, Lorraine Johnson."

It isn't uncommon for two people whom God has brought together to sense something special right from the start. Daddy wasted no time asking Mama out, and she eagerly accepted.

On one of their first few dates Mama heard Daddy speak at the Brea Nazarene Church. Her heart was deeply stirred by his impassioned words. God had obviously gifted him with an unusual ability to translate the Word into the common language of his listeners. She had never heard anyone dare to be so natural when preaching the Word of God, and she was understandably curious. Who was this forthright young man who presented the gospel without pretense or affectation?

The Pierce family roots lie deep in the soil of western Vermont, but my grandfather, Fred Asa Pierce, moved his family to the Midwest before my father was born. Grandpa Pierce was a widower with three daughters when he met and married Flora Belle Harlow Evison, a widow with two sons. Times were hard; Grandpa worked primarily as a carpenter, but he did other jobs when his carpentry skills were not in demand. It was no easy task to feed five hungry mouths, and the number grew with the arrival of Fred, Jr., and finally Bobby.

Daddy made his debut on October 8, 1914, in Fort Dodge, Iowa. He learned early the need to assert himself in a home where everyone was at least a head taller and twenty pounds heavier than he was. And he got his share of spoiling; Grandma always took a special joy and pride in her youngest boy.

When my father was still very young, the family moved to Greeley, Colorado, in an attempt to find relief from their financial difficulties. Even there it was a hand-to-mouth existence, but the more rural lifestyle made what they didn't have seem less obvious.

When my father was twelve, Grandpa gave up on Greeley and moved the family to Redondo Beach, California, where he took a steady job with the Safeway market chain. By this time only Freddie and my dad remained at home, and the little family joined the Grace Church of the Nazarene.

One of the pastors of Grace Church was Earle Mack, a deeply spiritual young man who immediately took a liking to my dad and went out of his way to encourage his involvement. Under Pastor Mack's ministry, Daddy made his own personal commitment to Jesus, a decision that not only secured his salvation but also proved to be a source of strength for days ahead. Shortly thereafter, Grandpa died of a strange, undetermined ailment.

Losing his father was a terrible blow for Daddy, but the loss was at least partially cushioned by his newfound relationship with his heavenly Father and by the wonderful people God brought into his life. His life became inseparably linked with Grace Church and its people, especially Earle and Ruth Mack. On Saturdays, church people would load into the "Gospel Car"—an old Ford truck they had converted to a bus— and rumble down to the corner of Manchester and Broadway. On most of those Saturdays, an earnest-faced boy of thirteen or fourteen could be seen standing on a soapbox, preaching his heart out to a good-sized crowd of passersby.

In college, Daddy was far better known for his outra-geous pranks than for any great spiritual or intellectual gifts. But while the faculty found him quite a handful, the other students loved him. In his junior year he ran as a "dark horse" for student body president and won. It was the most important and thrilling surprise of his life, until the night he met a brown-haired girl with gentle green eyes.

• • •

When Papa returned to Chicago, Mama stayed to finish the school year as a special student at Pasadena Nazarene College. Papa was well aware of the reason for Mother's sudden interest in a college education, but he wasn't hard to convince. He had dedicated Mama to the Lord, and he didn't believe the fulfillment of God's purpose for her life was waiting back in Chicago. Too, he was greatly impressed with my father, and if God wanted to do something with the relationship, he would do what he could to cooperate.

Mother's arrival on campus created quite a stir. Not only was she a rather glamorous addition to the conservative student body, but it quickly became apparent that she had taken one of the most popular men on campus out of circulation.

Daddy courted her with all the style his 1927 Model-A Ford and her seven-dollar-a-week allowance would permit. Frequently, Daddy would find himself temporarily financially embarrassed. But the school was on the side of a hill, and by coasting the old Model-A down the hill Daddy would be able to afford a ten-cent cheeseburger and still have enough gas to drive Mother back up to the dorm. Mama always knew what to expect when Daddy asked her out for a "coast" instead of a drive.

In the tradition of all great loves, Mom and Dad had their share of obstacles to overcome. At the time, Pasadena Nazarene expressed an extremely conservative attitude toward male-female relationships. Any public display of affection was prohibited. So when Daddy and Mama boldly held hands and even kissed goodnight on the dormitory steps, they soon received an invitation to the dean's office.

My father, who was never known for his diplomacy during moments of stress, let it be known in no uncertain terms that he didn't think Mother and he had done anything wrong. "If you think it is sinful for two people in love to hold hands, the problem is in your own minds, not ours!"

The poor dean of men and dean of women left with tears in their eyes at being talked to in such a manner. Mother was restricted to campus and forbidden to see Daddy again during the remainder of the semester.

That might have been the end of the story if it hadn't been for Papa's timely intervention. In response to Mother's plea for help, he wrote the president of the board of directors, and it was arranged for the couple to meet once a week at the parsonage for a closely supervised "date." After a few weeks of tea and cookies with the pastor and his wife, the restrictions were dropped, and Mom and Dad gratefully did their best to demonstrate true repentance.

The end of the semester meant a return to Chicago for Mother and an uncertain future for the young lovers. It was 1936, and the country was still struggling to recover from the Depression. Jobs were scarce, and Daddy had no recourse but to send Mama home.

Unwilling to say good-bye until the last possible moment, Daddy rode the old Union Pacific Challenger with her to San Bernardino, as far as his limited funds would allow. Those last few hours he held Mother's hand and talked confidently about the future. They had committed their relationship to the Lord, and surely he would bring them together again. And yet, Chicago was so far away. As Daddy waited by the roadside to hitch a ride back to Pasadena, he earnestly poured his heart out to the Lord. Only moments before, he had kissed Mama good-bye, and already he was aching to be with her.

His prayer was interrupted by the sound of a car coming down the road. With the casual expertise of an experienced hitchhiker, Daddy stuck out his thumb. Watching the car roll to a stop, he had an idea.

•   •   •

Back in Chicago, Mama moved in with her brother, Floyd and his wife, Marge. While Papa continued his evangelistic meetings, Mama found herself selling jewelry at Wieboldt's department store and living for the letters that arrived from California every day or so. The pain of separation grew more unbearable every day.

Just when she thought she couldn't stand it any longer, Mama received a letter instructing her to be home at nine the next Friday morning. Apparently Daddy missed her as much as she missed him, and he had decided to splurge and call her on the telephone.

The night before the expected call Mama couldn't sleep a wink. The morning sun found her wrapped in an old terry robe, her hair in curlers, her face dotted with cold cream, nervously pacing the apartment.

At nine sharp there was a knock at the door. You guessed it. Daddy's thumb had carried him clear across the country!

He stayed about a month, and he and Mother felt the bond between them deepen and solidify. But Daddy was only twenty-two, with no job, no money, and no apparent future. He couldn't stay indefinitely with Mother's friends, who had kindly given him a place to sleep. Soon it was time for him to make his way back home.

Mother said good-bye, not knowing when she would see Daddy again or even where he was going. He might hitchhike home, he said, or to his sister's in Santa Fe, or stop somewhere along the way if he found a job.

This uncertainty caused a major problem when Papa called a few days later to invite Mama and Daddy to join him for two weeks of camp meetings he would be conducting in Grand Rapids, Minnesota, a beautiful resort town. If Daddy would meet them in front of the YMCA in Minneapolis at six on a certain afternoon, he could be the song leader for the meetings. This would give the young couple precious time together.

It was the perfect answer to Mother's prayers, but how could she reach Daddy, who could be anywhere between Chicago and Los Angeles?

On a hunch, Mother felt led to write Daddy in Santa Fe. She didn't know his sister's address or even her married name, so the letter was simply addressed to Bob Pierce, General Delivery, Santa Fe, New Mexico.

A few days later, Daddy was aimlessly walking the streets of Santa Fe, praying and asking God to give him some clear direction for his life and for his relationship with Mama. As he walked, he noticed the post office across the street. No one knew he was in Santa Fe, but as he passed the post office he had an irresistible impulse to ask if he had any mail.

The look on Daddy's face must have been something to see as he incredulously took the envelope and checked to make sure it was really for him. The post office clerk probably talked for days about the strange young man who ripped open his letter, laughed out loud, and danced out the door shouting "Hallelujah" and "Praise the Lord" all the way down the street.

Daddy left Santa Fe with fifty cents in his pocket and only a few days to make it to Minneapolis. When Papa and Mama pulled up in front of the YMCA on the appointed day, they were astounded but delighted to find him waiting out front, freshly showered and shaved, a big smile on his face and two dollars in his pocket.

Safely settled in Papa's car on the way to Grand Rapids, Daddy described how he had prayed his way across country, trusting God to send him motorists who would pay him for driving while they slept. He never even missed a meal. Mama just shook her head in wonder and thanked God for taking good care of her unpredictable young sweetheart.

More months of painful separation followed Daddy's return to California. He worked at anything he could find—one month he killed rattlesnakes in the

Chevy Chase hills between Pasadena and Glendale; the next, he sold musical instruments through central California.

By November he had saved enough money to travel back to Chicago one more time. Mother was thrilled to see him and so was my Uncle Floyd. For months he had nursed his little sister through the emotional roller coaster she had been on ever since she met Daddy. In his opinion, enough was enough!

"For Pete's sake, why don't you two get married?" he asked one evening. That was all the encouragement the young lovers needed. That very night the evangelist's daughter married the carpenter's son in the Methodist parsonage in Crown Point, Indiana.

3 "A YOUTH AFLAME"

It would be nice to say that Mom and Dad hitchhiked off into the sunset and lived happily ever after. But even the movies don't try to sell that kind of fantasy anymore.

I strongly believe that the foundations of hell tremble every time a man and woman of God commit themselves to one another. The ministry potential of a couple yielded to the will of God is a threat Satan can't afford to ignore. In my parents' case, he was determined to defeat the troops before they had a chance to get on the battlefield. And he almost succeeded.

After a one-week honeymoon, Daddy decided he'd better return home to California and find a job to support his new bride. It was early December, and there was little hope that he could send for her soon.

Christmas morning found Mama still in Chicago, halfheartedly entering into the family festivities. As everyone opened presents, she saved Daddy's until last. Under the tree, the little box was almost lost among all the big, brightly colored packages. It certainly couldn't compare to the large, well-packed box she had sent him a week or so before.

As she tore off the brown paper and opened the small white box, Mother stared disbelievingly at the velvet jeweler's box inside. Daddy still had no job, and surely there was no money for this!

Her thoughts drifted back to a clear day the previous spring. She and Daddy had been strolling down Pasadena's Colorado Boulevard looking at the window displays and dreaming about the future. They had stopped to look at wedding rings in a jewelry store window and one ring caught Mama's eye—a delicate gold wedding band set with seven small diamonds. Now, fingers trembling, Mama slipped off the dime store ring she wore on her left hand and slipped on the simple gold band with seven small diamonds.

It was February before Daddy was finally able to send for Mother. Through Ruth Mack's father he had gotten a job laying hardwood floors. It was exhausting, difficult work. Daddy had to bend over at the waist for hours at a time, hammering nails down the length of one board and back the next. But the job was an answer to prayer, and he was grateful.

If she could have, Mama would have run all the way to California. Instead, her father offered to make the lengthy drive once again. The drive seemed endless, but finally she and Papa arrived in Glendale and checked into the hotel where Daddy was to meet them. Stationed at the window, Mama's eyes were glued to the street below, where any minute her Prince

Charming would appear. Up chugged the old Model-A. The door opened and out stepped Prince Charming, still in his work clothes, his hair escaping wildly in all directions from under his white painter's cap.

Mama felt a strange sinking sensation in the pit of her stomach as she recognized the young man she had married—a poor substitute for the romantic figure she had pictured the last few months. But as soon as he burst through the door and swept her into his arms, all her fears and reservations disappeared.

Soon after Mother arrived, however, Daddy's job ended abruptly, and he began drifting from job to job. None of them lasted very long, and Daddy's discontent grew greater with every new venture. He knew he had been called to the ministry, not to sell cars or insurance or to work in a bank. But he could not be licensed by the Nazarene Church because he hadn't returned for his final year of school.

At the same time, Mama struggled to adjust to her new life with the unpredictable young man she had married. She had fallen in love with a promising young preacher, president of the student body. He had seemed so sure of himself, so confident about the future. Now she found herself married to a young man who was seemingly going nowhere and who was taking her with him.

With romantic impracticality, neither Mama nor Daddy had considered the extreme differences in their personalities. Daddy's naturally impetuous spirit did little to foster the stability and order Mama wanted and needed, and she often found herself battling feelings of insecurity and doubt.

With few friends, no transportation (the old Ford had finally died), and only enough money each month to squeak by, there was little for the newlyweds to do but worry and argue. Finally, defeated and frustrated, Mama went back to Chicago for a visit. As she waved good-bye from the train window, she wondered if she would ever see Daddy again.

The weeks turned into months, and except for a few guarded letters, there was little communication between the two. Then one day Mama received a letter.

"My Darling Wife," it began. Mama's heart leaped at these words of endearment. The letter continued, and for the first time Daddy honestly shared his fears and frustrations. The last year had raised so many questions. Had he and Mother made a mistake? Why were things so difficult if God had ordained their marriage? Was he out of divine order? If God really had a sovereign plan for his life, where and how had he missed the boat?

One afternoon, the letter went on to explain, Daddy found himself standing on a street corner, unable to decide which way to go or what to do. Unwilling to return to the empty apartment, he stood for a long time watching the cars stop and go. The streetlight changed from green to yellow to red and back to green again.

The unending progression seemed to parallel his life at the moment—endless striving, going nowhere.

"Bob! Bob Pierce. Over here." He was startled from his thoughts by several old friends from school who were beckoning him to their car. "We're on our way to camp meeting. Want to come?"

The Nazarene denomination was holding its annual convention on the Pasadena Nazarene campus that year. Pastors and ministers from all over the country would be there, as well as many of his old friends. Daddy wasn't sure he wanted to face the old crowd, but it beat standing on the corner all night. So with a casual "Sounds great!" he jumped in the car and off they went.

It didn't take long for my father to recognize that it was no accident he was in the meeting that day. Everything seemed directed right at him, and the Holy Spirit dealt powerfully with his heart. Broken, rejoicing, and renewed, Daddy stood before the entire assembly and confessed with tears of repentance his difficulties of the past year, proclaiming with fresh conviction his determination to serve God. His testimony made such an impact that after the meeting several pastors sought him out and invited him to hold revival meetings in their churches. Doors of ministry flew open, and once again his direction was clear.

Daddy ended his letter, "I love you and want you with me. But whether you come or not, I'm going on with God."

It was the summons for which her heart longed. Mama's answer was short and to the point: "Yes! I'm coming!"

And so Mother and Daddy entered into their second year of marriage and their first year of evangelism.

Their first meeting was in San Diego at the University Avenue Church of the Nazarene, a large, prosperous congregation that welcomed them with expectancy and enthusiasm. Pastor and Mrs. South went out of their way to make the young couple feel appreciated and loved, placing them in someone's lovely home, graciously providing all transportation (Mom and Dad still had no car), and generally treating them like the biggest names on the evangelistic circuit.

God greatly blessed those first meetings. Every night the church was packed with people eager to hear the dynamic young preacher, and Daddy spoke with greater power and authority than ever before.

As his wife, Mother was both blessed and a bit overwhelmed by God's obvious anointing on Daddy's ministry. Night after night she watched as people crowded forward to respond to the invitation to receive Christ or rededicate their lives to Him. Convinced that God was going to do a powerful work through her husband, Mama began to battle feelings of personal inadequacy.

She had always been prepared to accept God's calling for Daddy's life. Part of the reason she loved him so much was because of his all-out commitment and desire to serve the Lord. But never before had she been so aware of what God was requiring from her, and suddenly she became conscious of weak areas in her own life—feelings of hurt and bitterness leftover from her parents' separation, and fears that had unconsciously put conditions on what she would allow God to do. Now he was challenging those conditions, and Mother was frightened.

One afternoon Mama knelt beside her bed, determined not to rise until she knew that all the questions were settled and she had total peace and confidence. Trusting the Holy Spirit to bring significant things to mind, she went through her entire life, confessing areas of sin and confusion. What Daddy had done publicly Mother now did privately. This was her Gethsemane, her place of dying to self. Unconditionally, she prayed, "Not my will, but thine be done."

Mother and Daddy left San Diego charged up and raring to go, and God blessed the twenty-three-year-old preacher. Churches all over southern California filled with people eager to hear, in the words of one handbill, the "flaming truths of salvation, in burning words from the anointed lips of youth." God gave him favor with young people, for whom he had a special burden.

As traveling evangelists, Mom and Dad were totally reliant upon the host church to supply them with food and lodging. Occasionally they were treated with the same hospitality and thoughtfulness they had received in San Diego, but those times were the exception, not the rule. In one town they stayed in a barn loft that had been crudely converted into a room with no bath. Another church provided them with a room and bath, but no running water. In yet another town they were informed that accommodations had been rented within walking distance of the church. They were greeted at the door by a walleyed old lady dressed entirely in black, her unkempt hair stuffed haphazardly under a wide-brimmed black hat, which she never removed. Each night Mom and Dad would come home to find the house dark and their landlady in the kitchen, surrounded by her five cats, rocking in front of the pot-bellied stove and strumming on an old guitar. Needless to say, they stayed only until a place a little less bizarre could be found.

These are experiences that are fun to remember, the kind you look back on and laugh at. But there were also genuinely painful experiences. My parents' only income was from the love offering taken during the meetings. It was never very much. In fact, at the end of the year Daddy figured they had averaged five dollars a week. But occasionally the Lord would touch people's hearts and they would give generously.

On one such occasion, the youth pastor in the church was so blessed by the congregation's response that he enthusiastically confided to Daddy the amount of the offering. Mother and Daddy were thrilled. But after the closing meeting the pastor handed them a check for fifteen dollars. Dumfounded, Daddy told the man that he knew the offering had been several times that amount.

Caught in an extremely uncomfortable position, the pastor exploded, "Why, you young whippersnapper, you don't need any more money than that. When I was your age, I would have been thrilled to have received that amount!"

Daddy firmly slapped the check back into the pastor's hand. "Here, you obviously need this more than I do!"

At times like that Mama couldn't help but wish Daddy were a little less impetuous and a bit more practical, but for Daddy the satisfaction was well worth the cost.

As difficult as this period was financially, it was a very precious time of growth for Mother and Daddy. To quote Mama, "I began to truly love your father during that year. We may have had nothing, but we had it together." Laughing and crying together, encouraging one another, learning to trust God together—all these priceless things established a root system, like that of a fine old oak, which was to sustain the relationship despite the raging storms and blistering droughts to come.

Thanksgiving was rapidly approaching, and Mother and Daddy returned to Los Angeles for the holidays. My grandfather had come out from Chicago several months before at Aimee Semple McPherson's invitation. God's blessing had attended his ministry at Angeles Temple so powerfully that Mrs. McPherson eventually extended her invitation from two weeks to thirteen months.

One afternoon Mama went shopping for Christmas cards. While she was out it started to rain, and her feet were soaked through her open-toed shoes. Later that evening she felt her throat getting scratchy and raw. By the next day her throat was so sore she could hardly swallow. Usually a sore throat was no cause for alarm, but for some reason Papa felt prompted to send for a doctor that very night. It took Dr. Matousek only five minutes to diagnose Mother's sickness as diphtheria. He immediately sent Daddy to buy some antitoxin, and within the hour Mama had received a massive dose of the life-saving medication.

Diphtheria can be deadly, and it is easily transmitted. Normally, Mother would have been taken immediately to the county hospital, where she would have been carefully isolated for two or three weeks of treatment and observation. But not wanting to relinquish his daughter to the care of an institution, Papa imposed upon Mrs. McPherson to use her considerable influence. Within the hour, the gracious lady had made the necessary calls and arranged for Mother to remain at home.

Each day Dr. Matousek would stop by to check on the patient, and Papa would stand at the door to reassure Mama of his love and prayers. But it was my father who tenderly nursed her, hardly leaving her side for the weeks it took the disease to run its course. It was Daddy who took her in his arms to comfort her when she cried out in delirium, who fed her, bathed her, changed her sheets, and emptied her bedpan.

Finally the crisis passed, and Mama began the long process of recovery. It would be a year before her full strength returned.

4 THE CENTER DAYS

Mother's illness put an end to that first year of travel and marked the beginning of "The Center" days.

"The church that radio built" was the way the July 1944 issue of *Radio Life* described the Los Angeles Evangelistic Center on the corner of Eleventh and Hope. Born of Papa Johnson's highly successful radio ministry, the Center seemed to spring into existence almost fully grown. God richly blessed my grandfather's ministry, and soon he gained a reputation as a great Bible expositor.

Every Wednesday and Friday night and three times on Sunday, the Center's lovely sanctuary was filled to capacity with people hungry to hear the Word of God taught with great simplicity, irresistible compassion, and unquestionable authority. At times, the power of the Holy Spirit charged the air like electricity, working physical healing. At other times the sweetness of his presence quietly restored emotional health and drew people to Jesus.

"Bob and I were absolutely submerged through those years in the message of the Cross," Mother recalls. "Papa loved the Word of God and made it come alive for us both. The Word of God became a lifestyle:

God said it, and we believed it, and it was that simple. Bob and I met life and death issues, and we survived because we believed God's Word."

Mother remembers the four and a half years Daddy was a youth pastor at the Center as some of the happiest of her life. During these years they had their first real home, a little apartment in Glendale. Although they furnished their home in "early orange crate" and "classic thrift shop," Mama loved every minute, and the two of them discovered many hidden talents. For instance, when she was pregnant with Sharon, she wanted a rocking chair, but every extra penny was needed to pay for the baby.

One night Daddy burst through the door, grinning boyishly from ear to ear. He proudly presented Mother with something that resembled a rocker, explaining he had rescued it from the back of one of the Center's huge storage closets. Mother hadn't the heart to point out that it had no seat and that one of the rockers had been practically rocked off. It wasn't exactly what she had pictured.

For the next few days, Daddy devoted every spare minute to refurbishing the old chair, using his carpentry skills to make a new seat and securing the wobbly arms and legs. By the time it was ready for sanding, Mother was caught up in the project. She tried her hand at sewing a seat cushion and a matching skirt. In its fresh paint and custom-designed dressing, the old chair became one of Mother's prized possessions.

Of course, much of the joy of those years was centered in the ministry. Mother and Dad worked together to build and sustain an effective youth program and evangelistic outreach, organizing mass rallies designed to reach young men and women for Christ. As an associate pastor, Daddy also had other responsibilities—such as leading the singing in the main services and doing his own radio broadcast every Monday night over station KMTR, Hollywood.

Music played a big part in my parents' life during this time. Mama always loved to sing and play the piano, and in his earliest years my dad was billed as an evangelist/singer. Now they joined their best friends, Riley and Flossie Kaufman, to form a mixed quartet. Mama also sang in the choir and ladies' trio, while Dad sang with the "King's Ambassadors," Papa's radio quartet.

I often heard Daddy call Papa Johnson his "seminary," for it was from Papa that Daddy learned many practical aspects of ministry. But far more important than learning the "how to" of ministry, God used Papa to open and expand my father's vision for ministry. Until this time, Daddy had never ventured beyond the Nazarene denomination. But at the Center, men of many denominational backgrounds came to exalt Jesus and proclaim the gospel, loving and accepting one another despite doctrinal differences. "Preach the Word, not the manual," my grandfather often said. It was a concept that released Daddy to feel comfortable in any church and with any group of people who honored Jesus Christ as Lord.

During these years, Mom and Dad met the great missionary statesman Dr. Oswald J. Smith. He brought the first real missionary challenge Daddy ever heard, depicting with heart-wrenching clarity the hopeless, aching need of a world without God. In those moments of revelation the soil was broken and the first seeds of missionary zeal planted within my father's spirit.

But for years Mother remembered that evening for quite another reason. At the end of the service a missionary offering was taken. Daddy, his eyes burning with visions of naked, starving people dying without ever hearing of Jesus, dug into his pocket, pulled out a small wad of bills, and dropped the entire lot into the plate as it passed. Speechless, Mother watched as their rent money disappeared down the aisle and out the door.

This was the first of many times when Mother questioned whether Daddy's irrepressible giving bordered on irresponsibility. She was torn between her conviction that paying the bills on time was pleasing and honorable in the Lord's eyes and her own desire to see the money used to ease suffering and spread the gospel. It took several years of seeing God always provide abundantly before Mother learned to rest in the assurance of Philippians 4:19: "My God will meet all your needs according to his glorious riches in Christ Jesus."

So the first years at the Center were busy and productive. God blessed, and Mother and Daddy grew—but Satan raged.

I suppose if she had been more discerning, Mother would have seen warning signals in Daddy's growing restlessness. Daddy battled feelings of dissatisfaction over his position at the church. It began to annoy him that Papa didn't give him a position of greater authority.

Another point of irritation was Mother's unusually close relationship with her father. In most marriages, time and separation naturally "cut the umbilical cord," but the close association at the Center seemed to give Papa all the advantages, leaving Daddy feeling like a poor second. Daddy deeply loved and respected my grandfather, but he was being eaten up inside by the need to prove his worth to Mother and to himself.

By April 1941 the battle within Daddy's spirit was intense. Mother was in her last month of pregnancy, looking forward to the arrival of her first child. Sharon surprised everyone by coming nearly two weeks early. Daddy came to the hospital every day after work to look at her and spend a few minutes with Mama. Then he would rush off to an evening service or to sing with the quartet on Papa's radio program.

One night when Mother tuned in the broadcast, someone else was singing Daddy's part. Confused and concerned, she tried to reach him. Failing that, she called Papa.

"Dad, I just finished listening to the broadcast. Bob wasn't singing. Is anything wrong?"

"I'm sorry, dear; we didn't want you to worry while you were in the hospital. Bob and I had an argument. He quit over a week ago."

Entering Mother's hospital room the next day, Daddy felt desperate and torn inside. How could he explain to her what he was helpless to understand himself? All he knew was that he was angry and frustrated and nearly overwhelmed by waves of rebellion. Like a swimmer floundering in the surf, he seemed unable to do anything to resist the tide of emotions that threatened to carry him away.

The following weeks were strange and unreal. Daddy was moody and uncommunicative, vacillating between guilt and anger. Only Sharon seemed to penetrate the shell into which he had withdrawn. Holding her close, he would bury his face in her little neck, inhaling her sweet baby fragrance. Other times Mama would discover him staring at Sharon as she slept. Mama couldn't be sure he knew she was there until he would finally slip his arm around her waist and whisper, "Thank you, Sweetheart."

Sharon was two months old when Daddy announced he was leaving. He had been invited to speak at a series of meetings up north, and he felt it would be a good time to think things through. When the meetings ended, however, Daddy didn't come home, heading instead for San Diego. His brother Fred lived there, and it would not be hard to get a job in the shipyards. He would be one man in a city of thousands. It would be a good place to lose himself—or maybe find himself.

As the days became weeks and Daddy sent no word, Mother was forced to acknowledge the truth. He was gone. He had walked out on her, on Sharon, and on his ministry. So she took Sharon and moved in with Papa and his wife Opal. With every passing day the uneasiness in Mama's spirit grew, twisting into an aching agony. The only place she could find any comfort or peace was in her prayer closet where she knelt in prayer for hours at a time. That was the only time she felt safe, the only time hopelessness and helplessness did not prevail. With childlike simplicity, Mama claimed the most basic promises of God: "And I will do whatever you ask in my name, so that the Son may bring glory to the Father" (John 14:13). "If you remain in me and my words remain in you, ask whatever you wish, and it will be given you" (John 15:7). Taking God at His Word, she claimed the restoration of her home and family.

One Wednesday night about six weeks after Daddy had left, Mama stood in the living room, staring out the window. She felt totally drained, beyond tears and words. In the quiet of that moment a voice spoke, saying simply, "I have heard. It is done."

Now Mama was not accustomed to having God speak so distinctly to her, and it took a moment to comprehend what she had heard. But the comfort and joy that flooded her soul convinced her of the reality of what had just happened. Laughing and crying, she rushed to call Papa, who was at Wednesday night prayer meeting, insisting they call him from the platform. "Dad, Bob's coming home!"

For the next few days Mama's feet hardly touched the ground. She lived in a constant state of expectancy, believing that at any minute the phone would ring or the door would open, and it would be Daddy. And so it was with a light step and a slightly pounding heart that she answered the doorbell the next Saturday afternoon.

"Are you Lorraine Pierce?" a strange little man asked.

"Yes."

"This is for you." Without another word, he handed her a white envelope and walked away.

Papa heard the cry all the way in the kitchen. He found Mama collapsed on the floor, holding her stomach as if she had just been kicked, hysterically crying "No, no!" over and over again.

Picking up the crumpled piece of paper, Papa read the court summons. Daddy was suing for divorce.

As the court date neared, and Mother and Daddy still had not seen or talked to one another. All communication had been between their lawyers. Both attorneys were highly sympathetic and truly desired to see the young couple reconciled. And so, when Mama requested to see Daddy just one time before going into court, it was arranged.

The first few minutes of the meeting were understandably stiff and uncomfortable. Finally Mother found the courage to crouch by Daddy's chair, forcing him to look at her.

"Just tell me one thing. Do you love me?"

Daddy's answer was unhesitating. "Yes."

"That's all I need to know. We'll make it."

"You don't understand. I've changed. I don't believe the way you do any more," Daddy said in obvious anguish.

Taking his hands in hers, Mama said, "Then I'll just have to have enough faith for both of us."

Mother and Daddy walked out of that office arm in arm, but the next year and a half continued to be a time of incredible testing. While Mama fought her battle in prayer and tried to be encouraging without appearing judgmental, Daddy continued his lonely warfare, seemingly unable to find the key that would release him from his spiritual torment.

He worked in the Los Angeles shipyards, scrupulously avoiding the church and all his old friends. Like the prodigal son about whom he had once preached, he had left his Father's house to taste of the world and had found it bitter and unsatisfying. Now he belonged nowhere. Once he had had it all—God's promises, a vision, a future. Now it was gone; he'd thrown it away. He'd hit the bottom, and the climb back up was too overwhelming to contemplate.

During this time Mother continued singing in the choir. Each Wednesday and Sunday night Daddy would drive her up, waiting outside in an inconspicuous spot until the service was over.

One Sunday evening in December 1942, Dr. Paul Rood, president of the World Christian Fundamentals Association, was speaking. From her place in the choir loft Mama had a clear view of the sanctuary. Dr. Rood was well into his message when one of the side doors slowly opened and a lean young man slipped into the back row. One by one the choir members recognized their former youth pastor. Many began weeping and praying as Dr. Rood ended his sermon and gave the altar call. Her heart bursting, Mother silently begged Daddy to respond. But as the service ended and the choir filed out, he was still sitting in the back of the sanctuary, apparently unmoved.

As Mother mechanically removed her robe, she tried not to let disappointment overwhelm her. God was still in control. She would just have to wait a little longer. She looked up to see one of her good friends standing at the door, her face aglow and tears streaming down her face.

"Lorraine, come quick. Bob's at the altar!"

To this day, Mama still weeps with joy at the memory of that night. Rushing into the auditorium, she was stunned to find Daddy not kneeling but lying across the altar, his body racked by gut-wrenching sobs of deep repentance.

It had been a year and a half since Mother had received the Lord's reassurance that he had heard her prayers—a year and a half of waiting and believing and holding on. Now the promise was reality. God had proven not only his faithfulness but also his omnipotence in a seemingly hopeless situation. It was a lesson Mother would remember and draw strength from many times throughout her life.

Next Sunday, Daddy stood before the congregation to testify of God's mercy and redeeming grace, contritely asking to be received back as "a doorkeeper in the house of the Lord."

Papa stood and, embracing him, said, "Son, we have no need for a doorkeeper, but we sure need a youth pastor. Welcome home!"

5 A SEASON OF NIGHT

Nearly two years of effective ministry followed my father's return to the Center, as God solidified and reinforced the deep work he had done within Daddy's spirit.

It was during this time that my father first tried his hand as a filmmaker. Borrowing a friend's movie camera, he and Mother set off to interview thirty of the world's best-loved hymn writers. The film was received so well that Daddy followed it up with one about successful Christian businessmen. From then on, his camera equipment was second in importance only to his Bible. In later years it would be an indispensable ally in depicting the great suffering and need of a world without hope.

The films completed, Daddy began to feel a new restlessness, and it soon became evident that it was God's time for Mother and Daddy to leave The Center. So when the Eureka Jubilee Singers, a popular black gospel group, invited Daddy to join them as their evangelist, Mom and Dad hit the evangelistic circuit once again.

Three-year-old Sharon especially enjoyed these months of travel. With her dark hair carefully arranged in finger curls and her bright eyes full of laughter and fun, she was the darling of everyone in her mini-mobile world.

While traveling in the East, Daddy heard about an exciting new work designed to reach youth. Youth For Christ (YFC) was just getting off the ground, and Daddy was tremendously encouraged to find other young men who shared his vision and burden to reach young people for Christ.

Attending the first YFC conference in Winona Lake, Indiana, Daddy was impressed by Torrey Johnson, the organization's founder and president. Torrey's dynamic magnetism attracted a whole band of enthusiastic young followers, including Billy Graham, Cliff Barrows, George Wilson, Bob Cook, Ken Anderson, and David Morken.

Shortly after his return to California, Daddy was contacted by a Christian businessman from Seattle. The Christian Businessmen's Committee of Seattle wanted to sponsor a YFC rally in their area, and they asked Daddy to direct it.

It was 1945 and thousands of lonely, sad-eyed boys in uniform roamed the streets of wartime Seattle, desperately searching for something to take their minds off the hell into which they would soon be sent. Separated from friends and loved ones, many found refuge in one of the bars or girlie shows that lined the busy streets of downtown Seattle. But others found their way to the Moore Theater, its neon marquee brightly inviting passersby to attend the YFC rally each Saturday night. Most wandered in out of curiosity or boredom, but once inside they were hooked!

With wit and contagious enthusiasm, Daddy endeared himself to each Saturday night crowd. He led them in joyous youth choruses, taking his mike into the aisles to catch solos from the audience. When he discovered which serviceman was farthest from home, he would invite the nervous young man to the platform, hand him a telephone, and tell him to call home "on the house." An expectant hush would fall over the crowd as the number was dialed and an unsuspecting "Hello?" was heard over the public address system. "Hi, Mom, it's me, Joe." The names would change, but the reaction was always the same—disbelieving stammering followed by shrieks of joy as, for a few minutes, a family was reunited by phone.

The evenings always culminated in a powerful presentation of the gospel. Many times Daddy would speak. Other times a guest speaker such as Billy Graham, Torrey Johnson, or Merv Rosell would deliver the message. In order to make it financially practical for these men to make the long trip, Daddy would arrange a week of meetings in surrounding towns. As a result, my parents spent two or three weeks each month traveling the "Pierce Northwest Evangelistic Circuit." Unwilling to do anything halfway, Daddy would borrow a truck, load it with sound equipment and a portable organ, and recruit local musicians to provide music for the services. The three- or four-car caravan would then make a whirlwind tour of the smaller cities between Seattle and Vancouver, Canada.

Daddy thrived on the hectic schedule, finding the constant demand on his mind and body exhilarating. But Mother found it difficult to define her position in the midst of the continuous hubbub. Daddy was constantly stepping up the pace, and Mama's efforts to keep up with him left her breathless and feeling that in some indefinable way she was losing him.

●　　●　　●

My folks had been in Seattle a little over a year when Daddy excitedly announced he had been asked to become YFC's vice-president-at-large. Mother was greatly impressed by the title until she learned what "at-large" meant—travel, travel, and more travel!

Sharon was ready to start school, and Daddy felt that since he would be gone so much of the time it would be best for his girls to be close to Grandpa Johnson. So the family prepared to move back to Los Angeles.

Several hundred people attended a lovely farewell dinner to express their love and gratitude. Mother knew she was expected to say a few words, a prospect that always left her palms sweaty and her throat dry.

But this particular night her nervousness seemed much greater than usual.

As the dinner plates were cleared and the speeches began, Mama felt her body begin to tremble. Her legs were shaking so violently that she began to doubt they would hold her weight. She sat rigidly in her chair, asking the Lord to keep her from falling flat on her face when she stood. And God was faithful. When the time came, Mother stood and graciously expressed herself, appearing perfectly poised and confident before the large banquet room of people.

Never before had Mother experienced such an extreme attack of nerves, but the incident was forgotten in the flurry of moving. Daddy was scheduled to start traveling immediately, school was starting, and there simply was no time to hunt for a house. So when someone told them of a house for rent, they took it, sight unseen.

The little house in Glendale proved to be old and badly in need of repair. The roof leaked, the pipes roared, and the floor was partially eaten through by termites.

Daddy had barely unloaded the furniture when he was off for an extended speaking tour of the United States. So, Mama put Sharon in school and tackled the enormous job of redecorating.

Endowed with her mother's fastidious nature, Mama was unwilling to paint an unscrubbed wall or settle for anything less than an exact match between the curtains and the wallpaper. Each night she fell into bed exhausted from the day's vigorous activities. Mother's frantic activity fairly screamed of the hysteria building up inside her. She lost herself in work, refusing to deal with her growing panic.

Ever since her youth, when she had watched her parents' relationship deteriorate, Mother's greatest fear was of being left alone. When she married Daddy, she had attributed his hunger for adventure to his youth. She was happy to share the excitement of travel and change until he found his niche and settled down to raising a family and pastoring a nice church somewhere. But Daddy's drive to keep on the go seemed to increase, not lessen.

Now with his new position, more separations were inevitable; the future promised nothing but one good-bye after another. Mama was unprepared emotionally to cope with the situation, and the demands of the move had exhausted her physical resources. Ever watchful, Satan grabbed the opportunity to strike a crippling blow.

The morning sun streamed through the bedroom window, bouncing off the freshly painted walls. Somewhere in the distance, Mother heard the insistent voice of her young daughter saying that if Mama didn't hurry she would miss her bus to school.

Mama had the strange sensation of being outside her body. She seemed to watch herself get out of bed, put on a robe, and walk unsteadily into the kitchen.

Pour the milk. Butter the toast. Wipe Sharon's mouth. Kiss her good-bye. Slam!

The sound of the closing door reverberated in Mama's ears. For a long time, she stood in the middle of the kitchen floor, her eyes darting from one object to the next as she desperately tried to find something familiar and safe. She became aware of the loud, uneven rhythm of her heart, its broken cadence carrying unnatural surges of adrenaline through her system to produce stomach-wrenching chills of panic.

Forcing herself to move, she walked into the living room. Sitting at the piano, she timidly touched first one key, then another, relieved to hear the notes ring out strong and clear. Next she moved to the typewriter, seeing each letter typed as irrefutable proof that she was a part of the world from which she felt so distant.

For the next couple of days Mama attempted to carry on. But finally the last string snapped, and she could go on no longer. Calling Papa, she was barely able to make herself understood as she sobbed, "Help me, Dad. I'm sick."

After a thorough physical examination, the family doctor could find nothing to explain Mother's strange symptoms. Against Mama's wishes, Papa sent for Daddy. He came home to find her frightened, disoriented, and unable to leave her bed. At a loss as to what to do, Daddy simply stayed close for the next several weeks, trying to be encouraging and constantly covering Mama in prayer.

During the nightmarish days that followed, Mama found God's Word the only antidote for her sickness of fear. Drawing strength from 2 Corinthians 10:5, she attempted to cast down "arguments and every pretension that sets itself up against the knowledge of God, and . . . take captive every thought to make it obedient to Christ." And Isaiah 43:2–3 promised: "When you pass through the waters, I will be with you; and when you pass through the rivers, they will not sweep over you. When you walk through the fire, you will not be burned; the flames will not set you ablaze. For I am the LORD, your God, the Holy One of Israel, your Savior."

After several weeks of complete bed rest and quiet, the fog began to slowly lift. Mother still couldn't face the world outside her bedroom door, but her body no longer felt like a throbbing exposed nerve, and she could tolerate an occasional visitor.

It was during this stage of her recovery that Torrey Johnson and another YFC evangelist came to visit. Seating themselves on either side of her bed, Torrey explained that YFC had been invited to hold a series of youth campaigns in China. It was an extraordinary opportunity, one that might never come again. But unfortunately, Torrey was unable to go. With a deep breath, he continued. "Bob refuses to even ask you himself. He knows how hard it would be for you to let him go. But I feel very strongly that he's one of God's men for this mission, and I'm taking it on myself to ask you. Please, Lorraine, release Bob to go to China!"

Mama's eyes registered the shock and disbelief she was feeling. Surely the man wasn't serious! She realized that no one truly understood the hell she had been through, but God did, and she was certain he would never ask her to face this alone. No! Absolutely not! It was too much to ask.

The next few days Mother agonized over the decision she had made. She knew Daddy wouldn't go without her consent, and she felt perfectly justified in not letting him go. Yet she had no peace inside.

She spent hours in prayer, searching her heart and waiting before the Lord. Finally, deep within her spirit, she felt God's answer. 'Trust me. Let me have him and let me show you what I will do for you."

Two weeks later, Daddy left for China.

6 CHINA CHALLENGE

Passport, visas, shots, last minute shopping and packing—the next two weeks flew by in a blur of activity.

Daddy needed to be in Shanghai by the second week in July for a series of meetings. In order to pay his way, YFC agreed to give Daddy some money from a rally they were holding at the Hollywood Bowl. As the end of June approached and the promised money didn't materialize, Mother agreed that Daddy should use their small savings to fly as far as Hawaii. Daddy was sure that by that time YFC would be able to wire him more funds.

But when he arrived in Honolulu, no money was waiting. Stranded, Daddy called only to learn that the expenses of the rally had devoured every penny and there was no money to send.

Finally YFC scraped up enough money to send my father as far as the Philippines. Landing in Manila, he was warmly greeted by John Sycip, president of a Philippine airline and also YFC's business representative in the Philippines. Dad was surprised to see a contingent of local newsmen also waiting to greet him. It seemed that, while he was a virtual unknown in the U.S., the fact that he was American made him something of a celebrity in the Philippines, and Mr. Sycip had arranged for him to speak to the Manila Chamber of Commerce the next day. Dad then boarded one of Mr. Sycip's planes and flew six hundred miles south of Manila to the island of Eohol. In a letter dated July 4, 1947, he enthusiastically described the response to a sermon he preached to a packed auditorium "with government officials all over the audience. At the invitation, sixteen were gloriously converted and over fifty more came on the call for consecration to service. So we're praising God."

The Philippines gave Daddy his first real taste of the tropics and introduced him to the beauty and fascination of the new world he was entering. In his letter he wrote:

> This country is fabulous. It's just like a dream. The people actually live in little thatched houses on stilts. And as I write now, across the street children play under the house, with a pig and a cow sharing the same shade with them. Of course, I'm getting all the pictures I can—I borrowed a movie camera for my stay here in the Philippines and am trying to get as much of a picture for you as possible.

> This Monday I leave for China, God willing. I expect to be two days in Hong Kong and then fly on to Shanghai.

Daddy flew from the Philippines to Hong Kong on one of John Sycip's planes. But he had never confided his financial need to John and he arrived in Hong Kong with only a few crumpled dollar bills in his pocket and no idea where he would stay or how God was going to get him to Shanghai. As he started to walk away from the plane, the pilot stuck his head out of the window and yelled, " I forgot to give you this!" A white envelope fluttered to the ground and when Dad opened it up, he found three hundred dollar bills. The pilot then pointed to a car and said, "Mr. Sycip has also arrange for a car and for your hotel. Good luck!" Later that day Dad would purchase his ticket to Shanghai for exactly three hundred dollars.

My grandfather loved to quote the old saying, "Faith steps out upon an empty void, then finds a rock beneath its feet." That's exactly how Daddy got to China—one step at a time!

While Daddy was experiencing God's faithfulness on his side of the world, Mama was receiving equally good care on hers. Although her physical and emotional battle continued, God constantly made his loving presence known through his Word, his people, and his unfailing provision. The China meetings provided great blessing but no income. While Daddy's needs were being met by periodic offerings from the States and other YFC funds, Mother and Sharon were cared for by a wonderful group of Christian business-men who believed so strongly in what God was doing through my dad that they were willing to help support his family.

During the next four months my parents kept the post office in business. My father's letters not only reported on his ministry; they also showed that his eyes were being opened to human need.

Shanghai, July 14, 1947

We have been worked almost to exhaustion. . . . Broadcasts at 7 AM every morning and night rallies every night in Shanghai's largest church, Moore Memorial Methodist—but God has gloriously blessed. Overflow crowds every night and about 900 saved these first six days. The missionaries seemed thrilled, saying they've never seen such results among youth here. And the crowd is 90% youth too. Glory!

What a country! You never saw such hordes of people. Living where they happen to drop at night. Whole families—mother, children, and babies suckling at the breast—all sleeping on the sidewalks, while thousands step around them. Filth, smells, and sweat—beyond belief. Yet many live in luxury. I can't describe it all but am trying to get pictures so I can show you when I get home.

Soochow, July 18, 1947

Glorious meetings last night—heavy rain before the meeting so only about 800 were present but almost 80 conversions. Hallelujah! The people are hungry, really hungry for revival. This morning's meeting was about twice as large as yesterday's and as I preached on the price of revival, there seemed to be mighty conviction. Oh, do pray for us, Darling; the need is so great, the field is so large, the opportunity enlarging before us constantly. More cities pleading for us to come. When Andrew Gih and I visited Shanghai's mayor at his office the day before yesterday, he offered the city's largest auditorium seating 4,000 if we will return in September. Other pastors made the same request. So we may arrange it, as universities and schools will be in session then.

Wish you and Sharon could walk the mile to church with me—narrow streets, masses of humanity everywhere. Everyone here curious about the foreigner, calling the one word they know—"Hal-lo!" Look in the shops—eight-year-old boys wielding sledge hammers ten hours a day, filthy hands chopping meat, chopping vegetables, scratching open sores, back to kneading bread. Little children, naked, urinating in the streets. Every mother with child suckling a breast, adorable babies. Skilled craftsmen making furniture, making metal pots, making shoes, making wicker, making clothes. Buddhist temples. Every step a rickshaw boy grunting for you to get out of the way. Every direction someone squatting with chopsticks, eating rice—oh, I give up. It's indescribable. I'm trying to capture it in the pictures, but that too is almost hopeless. . . .

You should see me. I'm laying on the bed, every window wide open, covered all over with red, itchy prickly heat, perspiring from head to toe. A spider the size of a dollar is crawling on the ceiling overhead, but I have never felt so needed in the Lord's work before in my life. And it is a glorious experience, all of it. . . .

The more Daddy saw of China, the more excited he became by the open, hungry hearts of the Chinese people.

Hangchow, August 3, 1947

God is blessing. This Is God's time in China and *if you were here*, I don't think I would want to leave. These people are *so needy, so hungry* for the Gospel that even a nobody like me can, under God, do *so* much that I doubt if I'll ever be willing to just "go through the motions" of evangelizing in America again. But I know one thing more. I need *you.* You *are* my partner and co-laborer together with God. And I do love you with all my heart.

And Sharon, Darling, Daddy is proud to hear that you are being a good girl. Help Mamma all you can, and keep praying for Daddy and China. I love you both more than life.

My father's reports confirm that China experienced a deep movement of the Holy Spirit during those twilight years, but he says little to indicate that he was aware of how fast the night was approaching. The dragon of communism was closing in, even as God continued to build and strengthen his church. he was providing China with an inner source of truth and hope against the day when the Bamboo Curtain would fall, shutting out all outside sources of Light.

Sian, August 8, 1947

Well, here we are, way out in the middle of old ancient historic China, a thousand miles from the security of the coast. The atmosphere is different here and you feel you are really a foreigner in a foreign country. A thousand years ago, near two thousand I guess, this was the capital of China. . . .

This has been the scene of much Communist activity. Eleven missionaries were massacred right here in the Scandinavian Alliance Mission in 1932; and in the area just six miles from here, there have been eighty-five Christian martyrs in the last eight months. You really begin to realize some of the missionaries' sacrifices when you get out here.

Nearby Communist activity did not dampen people's enthusiasm for the Christian meetings, however. Over twenty-two thousand people attended their last meeting in Sian.

In all probability this was the largest religious gathering in China in missionary history. The Chinese were packed in like sardines. Jammed in together with no aisles, no seats, no altar space; just one solid pack of hungry, ignorant, yet wonderful people. And they stood attentively for two hours and fifteen minutes. There was no way to call them forward, but conservatively, at least two thousand responded to the invitation, raising their hands high and earnestly repeating the sinner's prayer.

A week later, Daddy had big news.

Shanghai, August 16, 1947

We had the honor of a lifetime yesterday. Dave Morken and I had the privilege of being entertained by Madame Chiang Kai-shek in her own home here last night. She gave us almost an hour—something undreamed of by people here, and she was surely gracious. She is a woman of superb poise and charm. She is sharp as a needle, has a mind which grasps a picture in a moment. Her home here is an oriental dream, and she herself is most attractive. We told her briefly about Youth For Christ and she immediately showed interest, but Dave and I were a little disappointed at her lack of real spiritual insight. She rather thinks of Christianity in terms of Christian and social betterment, I fear. But she has had some real experience with God, I believe. . . . We tried to tell her of the power of the Gospel—and she agreed, saying that China's greatest problem was its "spiritual bankruptcy." I presented her with the Bible and she seemed genuinely moved, thanking me over and over again. Then Dave led in prayer and we left. Well, pray with us that some of the Scriptures and the testimony we left may be used of God in their lives. She and the Generalissimo surely need prayer.

From Shanghai it was on to Peiping, a city Daddy described as perhaps the most famous old Chinese city, full of beautiful palaces and temples. . . .

This is the home of China's most beautiful silks, and embroidery and lacquer carved boxes, too. The delicacy and beauty of the work is exquisite. All of China's silver jewelry, loveliest vases, best silks, etc. come from Peiping. So I have done *all* my shopping here. I believe you will love everything. . . .

The meetings have been glorious! And God seems to have given me unusual favor. The meetings are held in the largest church—again the Methodist. But all the churches—Presbyterian, Salvation Army, Assembly of God, Episcopalian, Plymouth Brethren, Congregational—all are cooperating. We have had hundreds standing. And best of all—over 1,000 conversions in the five days.

Daddy was always faithful in supplying statistics. His letter goes on to relate his schedule of meetings for the day and the glorious results: Spoke at girls' high school, 900 present, 175 at altar. Boys' high school, 1,100 present, 192 converted. Preached evening service, 1,700 present, 92 first-time decisions. He concludes, "In five days God gave me 711 at the altar for conversion. *All* of the glory belongs to Him! But I know you have a great share, too, Darling!"

Daddy's letters constantly reflect his awareness of the daily battles Mother faced and his appreciation of the considerable part she played in his ministry.

En route to Chungking from Shanghai he wrote a letter that Mother carried in her Bible for over thirty years. It began, "To be read whenever you are discouraged."

My Very Own Sweetheart and Co-Laborer in the Gospel,

At very best, no doubt, I can only dimly imagine the heartaches, the fears, the conflicts, the loneliness, the discouragements, the desperate battles you must face again and again—alone, save for our wonderful Lord. In tears again and again I have drawn aside to cry out to God for you. I am such a poor husband, and so inefficient and ineffectual both in my ministry to my home and my Lord, that it is a constant source of wonder that either of you care for me.

But my Darling, I am thinking of you constantly, and my heart is hourly mindful of the fact that you are paying a price, making a daily consecration, bearing a cross. Our loving Savior is noting it too. And it is the fact that these struggles are not easily won which lends them value in His sight. If the price was easy to pay, it would be no proof of devotion. So, do not be discouraged because you must battle to win. . . . It is out of our sufferings that we begin to discover our true motives. We discover whether we are serving self, or truly serving Him for His pleasure alone. . . .

Do not be dismayed if out of your suffering, my Precious, He prunes and digs about, sometimes painfully. I recall time and again the words you passed on to me from someone . . . "This painful experience too is from the loving Hand of God. It is the best and choicest gift His love can find to give you. If He knew a more generous token of love and care to present you, He would surely give it. This hard thing, this infirmity, this distress, this pain, is as much His *love* gift as was the richest pleasure He ever permitted you!"

These words have come to me again and again. Let them comfort your heart now, my Darling, "For it is God which worketh in you, both to will and to do of His good pleasure" Phil. 2:13. . . . So, my Darling Sweetheart, "Chin up!" We are on the winning side. And I'm proud of you. Proud of your fighting spirit for the Lord. Proud of your courage in the battle. Proud of the fact that out of all the better men in the world, you love me. And I love you more and more, every day I live.

Daddy arrived in Chungking with a swollen throat and lungs so congested that he feared pneumonia. He was physically exhausted and, in his own words, the excitement had worn off.

The city of Chungking did little to lift my father's spirits. It had been heavily bombed during the war, and for the most part it still lay in broken disrepair. Only one church building was left standing, and it was there that Dave and Daddy held their meetings. The little sanctuary only seated 300, but 102 people responded the first night and 60 the next!

From Chungking it was on to Chengtu.

Chengtu, September 9, 1947

My interpreter, Andrew Gih, and I are guests here in the manse of the Anglican bishop, and have never been treated more royally. The bishop, his dear wife, and the entire staff are some of the most genuinely spiritual people I have ever met. . . .

There was no way of evading the invitation to a Chinese feast given by the Methodist pastors this evening in my honor. They are the most generous hosts in the world, these Chinese! But I doubt if you would have enjoyed it. At all their meals everyone eats with chop sticks out of a common bowl.

Courtesy demands that you partake of everything. Tonight we had stewed eel, and frog legs, and sea slugs (like great big snails), together with stewed chicken, heads and legs and toenails all included in the stew. Very tasty, I must admit. . . .

In my last letter I told you I was going to speak in the great government high school in Chungking. Well, God gave us almost 500 who came out for Christ before the whole crowd! Oh, Dearest, this is the most wonderful harvest field in the world! And this is God's time! Missionaries have never seen it like this before! . . .

Two days later Daddy added this postscript:

We left Chengtu yesterday morning after a glorious climax to the meetings. One of the missionaries came to me at the close and said God had done more through our visit in three days than all the church and missionaries had done in a year. I do know God gloriously revived the whole city. New Bible classes are being founded in the universities to follow up the student converts. . . .

We've now had about 11,000 accept Christ! And they are really being followed up. They say that never in China has there been such enthusiasm over the follow-up work of personally contacting each one who accepted Christ. There

is no explanation of these things except that God
is sovereignly showing His power—"calling out a
people here for His name."

Daddy spent four months in China on that first trip,
and as the end drew near Mother looked forward to his
return with as much anticipation as he did. Each day
presented a fresh challenge of survival as she slowly
crept back to a semi-normal state. One week she would
overcome her fear of the telephone, the next her terror
of the supermarket.

People tried to be sympathetic, but when she
wasn't back on her feet in a few months, even close
friends were uncertain how to react. Most chose to
avoid the problem, quietly fading out of the picture.
Others decided that what Mama needed was a good
pep talk. "This has gone on long enough. It's time you
stop babying yourself and pull yourself together." But
when it became obvious that their well-intended advice
was not producing the desired results, they too backed
off.

And so this was a lonely and confusing time for
Mama. Her world was reduced to Sharon, Papa, and one
or two good friends who had suffered similar difficulties
and who knew what she was going through.

But although Mama had little emotional strength,
she had no problem coping with Sharon's daily
demands, constant though they were. Children have a
wonderful way of accepting people just as they are,

without pointing out their flaws and weaknesses. Mother never felt on the spot or pressured with Sharon and her little friends. Rather, she found their company refreshing and most enjoyable.

One day, while watching Sharon at play with a group of neighborhood friends, Mother had an idea. Calling the local Child Evangelism office, she arranged to open her home to neighborhood children. She used the Child Evangelism material and a flannelgraph board to teach the youngsters about Jesus. For years Mother was faithful to that ministry, starting a class wherever she moved and leading many precious little lives to Christ, including her own Sharon.

Daddy's absence was increasingly hard on Mother. One day while reading in Ephesians 6, it became quite clear to her that the only way she could continue to release Daddy and be victorious over loneliness and constant emotional attacks was to daily "put on the full armor of God so that you can take your stand against the devil's schemes" (v. 11). The power and reality of that Scripture verse impressed her so deeply that for years Mother began each day by kneeling beside her bed and mentally placing the "helmet of salvation" on her head, putting on "the breastplate of righteousness," girding her loins with truth, and shodding her feet "with the readiness that comes from the gospel of peace." Then, "take up the shield of faith, with which you can extinguish all the flaming arrows of the evil one," she felt prepared to face another day.

On his way home, Daddy had to stop in Winona Lake, Indiana for a YFC conference and he invited Mama to meet him there. Just the thought of being with him again endowed her with an energy and confidence she hadn't felt in months. And once they were reunited, Mother relaxed. She had been obedient, Daddy had gone to China, God had richly blessed, and now her long, lonely ordeal was over. Yes sir, the next time Daddy went anywhere she was going with him! And she did.

Youth For Christ was to hold its first International Conference in Beatenburg, Switzerland, with youth leaders coming together from all over the world. Mother and Daddy made the trip together, leaving Sharon with Grammy in Chicago.

The trip to Switzerland was a refreshing break for the young couple. They saw Europe for the first time together and enjoyed some much-needed time alone. But soon after their return to the States, Daddy began talking about returning to China. He had received many invitations to return for meetings, but his main concern was a film he wanted to put together. He had taken some footage the first time out, but he felt more was needed to complete the project.

Needless to say, Mother wasn't thrilled with the idea, but by this time she knew that asking Daddy not to travel was like telling an eagle not to fly. She also knew she could not interfere with what God was doing.

And so, in May of 1948, Daddy returned to China. On the plane he wrote:

"Darling, my memory of your brave good-bye and courageous strength all day Sunday has been inspiring to me. Never have I loved you so much! Never have I been so proud of you! Never forget for a moment that I adore you. I miss you, and after this trip, God willing, there will be no more long partings."

Kunming, May 31, 1948

Here we are at the end of our first city-wide campaign, and how our God has blessed and answered prayer! The city is 200 miles inland from Shanghai—it is the end of the Burma Road—a city of over a half million people. The meetings were held in the city's largest movie theater seating 1,500. We held two meetings nightly, one at 6 PM and the other at 8, and night after night more were turned away than could get in! The first night I preached the crowd was so great, those turned away almost started a riot and three people were injured, although not seriously. Police, with fixed bayonets, guarded all the doors every service after that—and in the five nights 1,300 people were at the altar for salvation. Hallelujah! Mission leaders said that probably more souls were saved in this campaign than in all the past twenty years in Kunming! Praise God!

Shanghai, Monday, June 7, 1948

God is continuing to bless. We spent two days up in Kuling, . . . the summer capital of China where the Chiang Kai-sheks make their summer home. I was invited to preach at a meeting in the Chinese Church. When I arrived at the church, the people of the community were slow in coming because the time announced was a little too early for them to get away from their work. When the captain in charge of Chiang Kai-shek's bodyguards arrived, the church was only partly full. He visited with me a few minutes and then suddenly disappeared. I was just getting ready to preach a little later, when in comes the captain with his entire company of soldiers marching behind him! He had gone back to quarters, commanded the men to fall in, whether they wanted to or not, marched them to the church, packed out the auditorium for me, and God gave me 19 of them at the altar to be saved, including the captain.

Interestingly, one of the most significant experiences in my father's life is not mentioned in any of his letters. This doesn't surprise me, as often it is only in hind site that we fully appreciate the significance of a decision or a moment that changes our lives forever. For my Dad, the chance to speak at a small girls' school on an island off of Amoy held no special significance at the time. But it was there that God would give a challenge that would eventually change the course of my father's life and give birth to ministries that would reach around the world.

The school was run by a group of Dutch Reform missionaries and it was their feisty, no-nonsense leader, Tena Hoelkeboer, who welcomed my dad and invited him to speak. My father gave the Gospel message in the simplest way he could, inviting the little girls to accept Jesus as their Savior. Many responded and as he frequently did in the States, he challenged the new converts to go home and tell their families that they were now Christians. The next day when he returned to say goodbye, Miss Hoelkeboer met him with a little girl in her arms. The child's back was bleeding from the beating her father had given her when she announced that she was now a follower of Jesus.

"This little girl did what you told her to do and now she has lost everything!" Tena fumed, thrusting the child into my father's arms. "So, what are you going to do about it?"

In an excerpt from Franklin Graham's book, "This One Thing I Do" my father recalled that moment:

"I stood there with the child in my arms. Tears were running down her cheeks. She was scared to death . . . shaking in my arms. She was heavy and my arms were getting tired. I was shaken to the core. . . . I had never been held accountable for any consequences of my message. Now I was faced with "Is what I say true? Is there any responsibility involved? Believe me, you do some thinking at a moment like that."

In the end, Daddy dug into his pocket and gave Tena the last five dollars he had and he promised to send more when he got home. But in years to come, as my father continued his journey of faith and saw even greater need, Tena's words would ring in his ears. "What are you going to do about it?"

7 THE WRONG DIRECTION

Bob Pierce was never the same after his trips to China. He went to China a young man in search of adventure, but came home a man with a mission. He was shocked and outraged that the extreme suffering and spiritual darkness he had seen could go unchallenged, and upon arriving home, he immediately set out to do something about it. Armed with the film he had taken, he traveled from church to church, proclaiming, "This is the reality of life for half the world's population—hunger, sickness, filth, poverty, death, topped off by total spiritual destitution." Then he would close with the razor-sharp challenge that still echoed within his own heart. "What are you going to do about it?"

Daddy intended to go back to China, but within weeks of his return to the States, the Communists overthrew the government, forced the missionaries to flee, and closed the Bamboo Curtain. I can only imagine his disappointment and confusion as a seemingly wide-open door was suddenly slammed shut in his face.

In an attempt to regain a sense of direction, he threw himself back into Youth For Christ, taking the temporary directorship of the Los Angeles rally. One day Daddy got an inspiration. Each year the famed Hollywood Bowl held an Easter sunrise service. Why not do something similar at the Rose Bowl in Pasadena?

It was just what he needed—a project to sink his teeth into. He anticipated a mighty work of the Holy Spirit as great as any he had seen in China! With his customary energy and imagination, Daddy set to work planning an impressive program that would insure a large turnout. Movie stars, Ralph Carmichael and his orchestra, radio spots, billboards—each day he had a new idea to explore.

Finally the day came, and as the Easter morning sky gradually blushed from a whisper of pink to a deep, dusty rose, cars lined up for six miles as twenty thousand people inched their way into the Rose Bowl parking lot.

Only God knows why things happened the way they did. Daddy may have gotten carried away with his own sense of style and his insistence on professionalism. Certainly the program was planned not only with great care but with much prayer. And God received his offering, allowing this Easter sunrise service to become a Pasadena tradition for over twenty-five years. But when the offering was counted, Daddy found himself $6,000 in debt.

The Rose Bowl fiasco was a staggering blow, and it marked the beginning of another walk through the valley for my parents. The initial sting was so painful that Daddy disappeared for a few days, unable to face his family and friends. When he finally surfaced, Mother whisked him off to Palm Springs to lovingly comfort and encourage him and to help him sort through his feelings. His anger needed to be faced, and the feeling that God had let him down had to be confronted and confessed before healing could begin.

Palm Springs provided my folks with a much-needed rest. But Daddy's problems weren't finished yet. In the summer of 1949, Daddy received an invitation from the Kilbournes, Oriental Mission Society (OMS) missionaries he had met in China, to come to Korea. Daddy's immediate response was positive, partly because of his memories of China, but also because a deep stirring within his spirit told him he was supposed to go.

On the other hand, Mother had no such stirrings, and she seriously questioned the necessity of the trip. She had just discovered she was pregnant with me, and she didn't relish the idea of being left alone for an indeterminate period of time without any reliable income or the support of Daddy's presence.

But the conviction that he was called to go outweighed Daddy's sense of obligation to his family, and despite Mother's objections he left on a YFC tour of speaking engagements, hoping to raise money for his trip. Two weeks later he was back, frustrated and deeply discouraged. YFC's most effective fundraiser was now unable to raise the money he needed for himself. A small amount had been pledged in different meetings, but it wasn't enough.

In the end, it was my mother who got the rest of the funds Daddy needed. Still dreading the separation but sensitive to the signs of God at work, she got the money from a friend. Mama's only request was that Daddy return as soon as possible.

Things started to go haywire the day Daddy announced he was going to Korea by way of Paris, France. For reasons I have not been able to ascertain, his camera was in a repair shop there, and he needed it for his trip. Mother quickly pointed out he'd be going in the wrong direction. It would probably cost less to buy a new camera than to fly to Paris. But Daddy was adamant and off he flew.

Paris proved troublesome from the very beginning. When he arrived at his hotel, Daddy discovered his reservation had been lost and no rooms were available. However, he was able to locate a small room at another hotel. Next, he found, that the only person who knew where his camera was no longer worked where he could reach her. It took two days to track her down. Finally, camera in hand, Daddy prepared to leave for Korea by way of Cairo and Bombay . . . "as soon as the camera is cleaned and fixed."

A letter dated August 6 begins: "Boy, is Paris a jinx!" First, the camera repair was delayed. Then he was put flat on his back with the Parisian version of Montezuma's Revenge. Nauseated, weak, depressed,

Daddy wrote on August 11, "Each day I've been sure I would be better and on my way. . . . But, Darling, I've really had a time."

He goes on to describe repeated problems with his camera, and his discovery that in order to take film into India he would need to put up a cash bond. Everywhere he looked there were problems, and his sense of isolation increased as the days passed and he had no letters from home. For while Daddy sat delayed in Paris, Mother was sending her letters on to Bombay.

His last letter ended: "When I don't hear from you, it's hard on me not to know how you are feeling and if all is well with you and Sharon. I'm praying daily that all is well. . . . Oh, how I hope you've written so I'll have a letter in Bombay."

Daddy never got to Bombay to receive Mama's letters, and one day his letters to her stopped coming. He alone could explain just why and how the bottom dropped out, but somehow he had once again lost contact with God's purpose for him.

In the meantime Mother waited at home, her concern approaching panic as the days passed and Daddy's silence continued. Assuming he had gone on to Bombay, she finally wired the American embassy there to see if her letters had been picked up. But before she received an answer, a friend called to say Dad had been seen in Paris. An acquaintance had run into him in a camera shop. Their conversation had been awkward and brief, but the message had come through loud and clear. He had given up, and he wasn't coming home.

I know it's hard to understand how the author of the letters you just read could find himself in such an unGodly predicament. But then, how could the children of Israel rebel against God and build an idol in the wilderness after witnessing the parting of the Red Sea and being fed every day by manna from heaven? And how could David—a man after God's own heart—stoop to such treachery and deceit to obtain Bathsheba as his wife?

Obviously God is not dependent upon our perfection to get His work done; rather, we are dependent upon him to work wholeness and health in us so that his Spirit can work through us in purity and power.

Perhaps God was giving Daddy some rein to remind him of his own fallibility and to refresh his awareness of the source of his strength and ministry.

"God gently leads His children along. Me, He yanks!" Daddy used to candidly observe. No one was more aware than he that his iron will constantly needed breaking. As a child, I often heard my father pray, "Lord, I give you license to interfere in my life any time you see me going the wrong direction. Slam doors, knock me down, do whatever you need to do, but have your way."

And God did. But sometimes he used dramatic and frightening methods to do it!

For the second time in her life, Mother entered into spiritual travail. The news that Daddy wasn't coming home confirmed her worst fears and left her once again with no recourse but prayer. Spending hours on her face before God, Mama reminded him of his many promises. The growing life within her was a constant reminder of the love she was in danger of losing. Her emotional buffers weakened by her physical condition, despair would engulf her at times, leaving her sobbing wordlessly before the Lord, depending on Romans 8:26: "We do not know what we ought to pray for, but the Spirit himself intercedes for us with groans that words cannot express."

Finally, the intensity of her spiritual travail threatened to bring on physical labor. She began cramping, and Papa rushed her to the doctor. After giving her medication and ordering complete bed rest, the grim-faced doctor took Papa aside. "Better get Bob home fast, or she'll lose that baby!"

Papa succeeded in cabling Daddy in Paris. The realization that Mama might lose her baby was enough to bring Daddy home, but the problems and doubts came with him. My parents' communication had broken down, and suddenly two people who had shared the deepest intimacy had nothing to say to each other. They found themselves on either side of a raging river of hurt, accusation, and misunderstanding. Neither dared to step out too far for fear they would be swept away by the current.

There is no dramatic climax to this portion of the story. No instantaneous miracle occurred, but there followed a slow, gradual period of recovery. As the months passed, Daddy inched his way back into a comfortable relationship with his heavenly Father. The closer he got, the better things were between him and Mother.

In the meantime, the two did their best to reassure Sharon. At eight, she was keenly aware of the fact that things were changing, and her ear was constantly tuned to the tick, tick, tick of the emotional time bomb she hoped would never go off.

Christmas was coming, and since Daddy hadn't worked for a while the cupboard was pretty bare. Sharon had excitedly asked Santa for a bicycle, but there was barely enough money to pay the rent that month. Christmas morning dawned to reveal a shapely little Christmas tree bravely displaying a scattering of balls and a few small packages carefully placed beneath its boughs. Sharon entered the living room with studied cool, but she couldn't quite hide her disappointment when she saw no package larger than a shoebox. With a resigned little sigh, she sat down to open her presents— jacks, a box of paper dolls, new panties, a pair of socks, and of course, the annual bedroom slippers.

"Sharon, would you get my sweater out of the closet?" Mama asked ever so casually.

As she opened the closet door Sharon froze. With eyes big as saucers she stared at a beautiful, fire-red two-wheeler. The house was filled with her delighted screams and with my parents' equally delighted laughter. So what if things would be tight for a while? It was a small price for their daughter's joy.

That bicycle was to come in handy soon. A recent accident had demolished the car, so when I made my appearance in January, Daddy pedaled to the hospital to visit us, balancing Sharon on the handlebars.

My arrival seemed to mark the end of Daddy's spiritual detour. In March of 1950, he prepared again to make his first trip to Korea, finally headed in the right direction.

8 BIRTH OF A VISION

My father had no special sense of destiny as he boarded that plane for Korea. He went there as he had gone to China, to preach the gospel. It had been arranged for him to hold a series of campaigns throughout South Korea with Gil Dodds, an Olympic gold medalist.

A typical day for my dad might begin as early as 6:30 AM, when he would preach to soldiers at an army camp chapel. Then he would go on to a girls' high school for a 9 AM meeting, a 1 PM high school assembly for boys, a 3 PM assembly for teachers and faculty, and a 7:30 PM service in the city's largest auditorium. In between meetings, Daddy might stop to visit a colony of lepers living among the tombs of a cemetery.

On such a typical day, Daddy would speak to four to six thousand people, seeing hundreds come to know Jesus. He described one invitation this way. "When I called them forward it was like a dam bursting— glorious!"

Daddy wrote that during a seven-day campaign in Taegu, more than fifteen hundred received Christ. On the last day he spoke at the Bible Institute. "God poured out His Spirit in such power that classes were suspended for the rest of the day while students went to prayer," he wrote.

From Taegu the campaign moved to Pusan, and then on to Seoul.

> Seoul, April 18, 1950
>
> It is only 7:30 AM, and I have just now preached to 2,000 people. God is gloriously blessing, and last night we saw our greatest altar response yet. Monday night it rained and we could only get a small part of the crowd under shelter. But our crowds have been running larger than 16,000 each night.
>
> We are all being worked to death. For days I have been going from 6 AM till midnight without rest. However, today and tomorrow I will only preach three times a day, and so can rest a little. Then I'll travel by train to the President's Assembly in Taegu on Friday and begin preaching there for one week on Saturday. It is a crucial hour in the church and their one hope is revival. Pray much for me.

The meetings in Korea came to a marvelous climax in the city of Inchon, where they had crowds of almost fifteen thousand each of the last four nights, the largest on record. Reports from the cities where they had their first meetings began coming in, and it was not uncommon for a pastor to report as many as 250 new members in his church. When Daddy left Korea, a great crowd swarmed to the airport to see him off.

By June 1, Daddy was home, safe and sound. Again he had incredible stories to tell and reels of film to show. But within a matter of days, the stories were academic and the film outdated. Communist troops crossed the Chinese border into North Korea, and the little country literally exploded into war.

First China. Now Korea. Daddy certainly had a knack for narrow escapes! But he was deeply concerned about those he had left behind—missionaries and pastors he had worked with and had grown to love during his time there. And what was happening to the church, to the thousands of Korean Christians who would rather die than deny their faith?

Hours after hearing the news, Daddy was in Washington, D.C., pulling any string that happened to dangle within his reach and cutting through miles of red tape in order to obtain permission to return to Korea. Absolutely no civilians were being allowed into the country, but by arranging to file stories with the American Christian Press he could get in as an accredited war correspondent. The title gave him the rank of an officer and the right to fly with the military. Upon returning to Korea, he was horrified to discover his worst fears being realized. This clipping from a December 30, 1950, Akron, Ohio, newspaper partially describes what he found.

Dr. Pierce said the Korean War already had cost 80 per cent of the Christian leaders in North Korea. The Reds have extended their exterminating tactics wherever they have gone, he said.

He told of 47 leaders in Seoul tricked into assembling in one of the large churches by promises of cooperation. They have not been heard of since, said Dr. Pierce.

"One afternoon 3,000 Christians were murdered on the banks of the Han River, their hands bound by barbed wire," said the missionary.

He said 24 pastors were killed in the small town of Sonchon.

"I have testimony to this on my wire recorder," said Dr. Pierce, "from a man who escaped the Reds by burying himself for seven days under the filth of a pig pen."

He said a huge pit in Korea held 1,800 bodies of persons killed because "they went to church."

He appealed for funds, for tracts to be distributed to the Koreans, for medicine needed by Korean lepers, and for the orphan children walking in the snow.

That brief clipping gives only a glimpse of the horror and pain Daddy encountered. If these homeless, terrorized, desperate people didn't become innocent casualties of the war that exploded all around them, then starvation or disease stood ready to fell them. If somehow they managed to scrounge enough to eat, they still had to contend with the icy winter. Someone else might have been defeated at the onset by the magnitude of the need, but for my dad it was a call to battle. And one of the major weapons of that battle was his camera.

Back in 1948, when Daddy returned with his China footage, he had formed Great Commission Films with a young filmmaker named Dick Ross. Daddy shot the film, then Dick edited it and put it together. Together they produced *China Challenge, Dead Man on Furlough, The Flame, This Gathering* Storm—films which went far beyond the typical missionary presentation, since Dick was a talented professional whose demand for perfection equaled my dad's. By the time Daddy got home from his second trip to Korea, Dick was already hard at work on that early Korean footage. The result was an emotion-packed film entitled *38th Parallel.*

It was one thing to stand before a group of well-fed, healthy people and describe the hell others were experiencing. It was something else to show them. *38th Parallel* brought people face to face with the atrocities of war and the unconscionable suffering of the innocent—whole cities constructed of cardboard and newspaper; families huddling together in a feeble attempt to find shelter from winter's savage elements; thousands of dark-eyed, helpless children, their ballooning stomachs a stark contrast to their toothpick arms and legs; a young mother tenderly embracing a tiny bundle, the child's weak cry leaving no doubt that soon her arms would be empty.

Night after night Daddy presented his appeal and people responded. Money came pouring in, and it became obvious that some kind of organization was needed. Prayerfully, Daddy sought the Lord for direction.

• • •

In September 1950, World Vision became a legal corporation with Bob Pierce as president, Paul Meyers as vice-president, and Frank Phillips as executive secretary. It was formed as a missionary aid organization to meet needs during times of crisis in the Orient, and it was headquartered in Portland, Oregon.

World Vision's initial priority was simply keeping people alive, so it provided food, clothes, blankets, and medicine for the thousands left homeless by the war. In 1951, Daddy was touched by the plight of the women in the Tabitha Widow's Home, sponsored by the Yung Nak Presbyterian Church in Seoul. Soon World Vision was responsible for its support.

As the war progressed, another problem began to materialize—the GI baby. Considered outcasts by Korean society, many of these precious little ones were simply left to die in the streets. Some mothers tried to care for their illegitimate offspring, but when the fathers were transferred or shipped home, there was no way to support the children, and so they perished. Many were brought to one of the World Vision children's homes that began springing up throughout Korea. At first there were thousands of children and no organized method of sponsorship.

One evening in 1953, Daddy was speaking to a large congregation in the States. Afterwards, a young boy in his mid-teens approached my dad with a big grin and said, "You probably don't recognize me. I'm—"

With one of his world-famous bear hugs, Daddy embraced the boy. "Of course I do! You're Erv and Flo Raetz's boy." Daddy had met the Raetzs in China, where they had run a child sponsorship program for the Christian Children's Fund. "Where in the world is your father? I have a job for him." A few months later, Ervin and Florence Raetz went to Korea to set up a child sponsorship program for World Vision. In 2004, as I write this revised edition, World Vision is the largest sponsorship program in the world, with over 2.2 million children sponsored around the world.

Another burden my father had was for the many pastors who were forced to flee the Communist invasion of North Korea. Having lost everything, these men bravely struggled to recover some sense of direction for themselves and for the Korean church at large. In order to unify and strengthen the church, World Vision held a pastors' conference. Its success soon led to conferences in Formosa, Vietnam, the Philippines, and eventually in other countries around the world.

World Vision supplied hospitals, clinics, leprosariums, schools, and churches with medical equipment, jeeps, buses, trucks, and wheelchairs—and this is just a sampling of the services they provided. And the driving force behind it all was the compassion, the energy, and the vision of one man. In fact, to most people World Vision *was* Bob Pierce.

Within a few short years, his inexhaustible efforts made him a legend throughout the Orient. No need was too great for him to tackle or too small for him to bother with. My father never set limitations on his ministry or on God. He thoroughly enjoyed watching God accomplish the impossible and learned never to think too small. "Always leave room for the 'God space,' so that after you have done all you possibly can, God has room to work," he used to say.

Missionaries loved him because he made them feel their significance. Despite his grueling schedule, he found time to get involved with their lives, to sit at their tables and know their families. Daddy loved these people; in many ways he felt more at home with them than he did with us. They were on the same team, having a common call of God on their lives. They needed and drew strength from one another.

Between 1956 and 1964, Daddy would become one of the ten most traveled men in the world, receiving one- and two-million mile certificates from several different airlines. The walls of his office would be lined with awards, plaques, and testimonials for the work he had done. He would learn to be at ease with presidents and kings as well as with lepers and jungle tribesmen.

But no one could have predicted these things in 1950 when World Vision opened its tiny office in a corner of YFC's offices in Portland, Oregon.

•   •   •

I have no memories of my father during the three years we lived in Portland, partly because I was so young and partly because he was seldom there. World Vision and I were born the same year, and she was a much more demanding baby than I. I do remember the special time each evening after dinner when Sharon, Mother, and I would kneel by the living room sofa for our family devotions. Those times on our knees not only were spiritually significant; they also helped bind us to Daddy in a tangible, positive way. As we entered into this ministry through prayer, the family was united and solidified, and we were made conscious of the fact that we belonged to one another.

Mother did a beautiful job of keeping Daddy involved and a part of us. Shortly after we moved to Portland, my folks bought a machine that enabled them to make their own records. It was a rather tedious process, but in my mother's opinion it was well worth the trouble. In this way she could capture precious moments Daddy otherwise would have missed— birthdays, holidays, family gatherings, Marilee singing

"Jesus Loves Me" at eleven months, Sharon's first piano recital, thoughts and feelings and expressions of love that most wives share with their husbands in the quiet moments after the children are in bed but that are seldom remembered in the morning.

There is no denying that the Portland years were tremendously difficult for Mother. While I grew from an infant to a toddler, she struggled to adjust to "marriage by correspondence." Complications after my birth had left her physically weak and vulnerable. Old fears began cropping up, and new attacks of nerves often left her hands clammy and her stomach queasy. But her greatest battle by far was against the constant, aching loneliness. During that time Daddy was gone an average of ten months each year, a statistic that would vary only slightly during the next fifteen years.

There was never really any question that Daddy should go. The conviction that he was under divine commission to do exactly what he was doing far outweighed the yearning of Mother's heart. But that didn't make it easy for her to let him go; letters were poor substitutes for the sound of her husband's voice or the feel of his arms holding her close.

One particularly nice thing that happened in Portland was my parents' reunion with Earle and Ruth Mack. They were living in the area, which made it possible for Mother to go with Daddy occasionally, leaving Sharon and me in the Mack's loving care.

But even with the Macks close by, Mother's physical condition didn't allow her to travel much. Daddy's work in Korea had opened doors of ministry worldwide, and when he was invited to hold a series of campaigns in England and Ireland in March of 1952, he decided to take Sharon with him.

Mother was thrilled that Sharon had the opportunity to go, and she had no doubt that she would make her father proud. Still, it wasn't easy to stand at the gate and watch her ten-year-old march across the field and up the stairs to the plane.

For Sharon, arriving in England was like stepping into fantasyland. Buckingham Palace, the Changing of the Guard, the Tower of London, the Crown Jewels— wonderful things thrilled her eyes and aroused her imagination.

On the Saturday before they were to leave London for Belfast, Ireland, to begin Daddy's campaigns, Billy and Ruth Graham invited them to the Savoy for lunch. "We arrived to be royally greeted by all of them," Daddy wrote. "Billy, Ruth, Cliff and Billy Barrows all made much over Sharon. Cliff immediately took her and bought her a corsage. We had a marvelous time."

Then it was on to Belfast, where Daddy described the campaign as "only four days long, but one of the best I've ever had." Every night the auditorium was packed with over three thousand people, and at the end of each service dozens came forward, although "here

105

they do not believe in coming forward. So it is really phenomenal that we have had such results."

While in Belfast, Daddy and Sharon were guests of Major Neill, a member of the Irish parliament and minister of labor in the national cabinet. They also had tea with the prime minister. On the last night there, Sharon gave her testimony in the service, and Daddy wrote back that she did "gloriously." He added: "The people really took her to their hearts. She is a marvelous trooper!"

The next series of meetings was scheduled in Liverpool, England. It was from there that Mother received a letter from Sharon.

> Last night Daddy started the Liverpool campaign. It is being held right now in the Philharmonic. Last night we packed it out and turned people away. I think that is the way to start a campaign, don't you? I have been giving my testimony lots of places and have stumbled on my words quite a lot in front of small audiences, too. But last night I gave my testimony in front of a huge crowd and didn't feel nervous or scared, but right at home. I didn't stumble either. I said, "I am very glad to be here tonight and I love the Lord with all my heart and I have wonderful peace and joy since He has come into my heart." How do you like that?

As elated as Sharon was over her trip, no one was more thrilled than my dad at the opportunity to show off his charming daughter. He wrote:

I am sure that Sharon has never been happier in her life. She continues to eat like a horse, and she is having a good time in the meetings, too. Last night she signed autographs for twenty minutes. In fact, in every city now she has been mobbed just like the rest of us, and does she love it! She signs some Psalm verse after her signature like an old trooper. Everyone everywhere compliments us on her manners and pleasant little ways. So, I guess you gather from that that I am terrifically proud of her.

The meetings are going along splendidly. As you know, the first night England's finest opera house seating 2,500 was packed and hundreds turned away. . . . We are going to move to the Boxing Stadium seating 4,000+ beginning Saturday night.

My heart is full of His praise. And, Darling, never, never have I loved you more.

By May, Sharon was home and settling back into the routine of school and family life. But Daddy's routine was airplanes, hotels, strange food, and one service after another. From the jungles of Formosa to the World Congress in Ireland, from the war-torn streets of Korea to the crowded streets of India, the schedule never let up, and neither did he.

Although she was seldom able to be at Daddy's side, Mother didn't let distance prohibit her active involvement in his ministry. When she would hear of something she could do, Mother would make it her own special project. Such was the case with the sewing machines.

Perhaps in a letter or in conversation Daddy mentioned that if the women in the Tabatha widows' home in Korea had some sewing machines, they could earn enough money to live by sewing clothes and uniforms. Mother immediately set out to raise enough money to buy the needed machines. Despite the fact that speaking in public had never been easy for her, she called churches in the Portland area, arranging to speak to several women's groups. With Auntie Ruth at her side as moral support, she spoke as a woman and a mother about the desperate need of these Korean widows to provide for their children.

In a few months, Mother raised enough money to buy eight new sewing machines. And so she continued her battle behind the lines, doing what she could to help while Daddy was facing spiritual artillery, but also real guns and bullets.

Seoul, September 1, 1952

Today we went to the front, right up into the action. Ninety men were killed here in one day recently. Both sides are so close to each other that men are being killed by hand grenades and sniping daily. We donned armored vests and helmets and got a close view—so close I personally got a glimpse of three of the enemy.

. . . However, don't worry, I take no chances. Mostly staying underground in the bunkers, and watching through periscopes.

Daddy got out of the bunkers without a scratch, and the beginning of 1953 found him in Calcutta, India.

Calcutta, February 1, 1953

God continues to gloriously bless here in the meetings. Dr. Corlett, pastor of the leading church in the city, said in his pulpit this morning that Calcutta has never seen anything like this moving of God's Spirit, nor crowds like these in all the memory of the oldest missionaries.

There are some conversions among the hardest people to reach. Last night a turbaned, black-bearded young Sikh came forward and was graciously saved. My heart is so grateful. This whole experience is like a new beginning for me. I don't know how it is happening, but oh, how I thank Him! How I love Him! And somehow I've been pleading with God to let some of this joy and victory come through to encourage your heart. Day and night I am praying that God will do something to set you physically and spiritually free to experience these thrills with me. How glad I am, now, that I hung on to get there. I tremble to think that except for God's faithfulness when I was without faith, I would have turned back.

One of the most extraordinary episodes in my father's life was his ministry to the soldiers and POWs during the Korean War. In June 1953, he wrote:

> Here I am in the heart of the war prison camps. . . . We have been told we are not going to be allowed to participate in the camps and are awaiting an appeal. I hope you are praying. But whether I get to preach or not, here is one of the greatest Gospel stories in the world. In one big camp here, the Korean pastors have organized the Christians among the prisoners, and there are six churches now meeting in this one camp. Most amazing of all, they have their daybreak prayer meeting every morning, and even the unsaved attend, with often as many as two and three thousand present. Yesterday morning in a nine o'clock weekday preaching service, there were 60 decisions for Christ among these Communists. There are six Bible schools among the prisoners, with over 1,000 students studying the Word.

The prayers of my mother—and others—were answered when Daddy was allowed to preach to thousands of Communist POWs.

> I have spent my first weekend among the prisoners of war—hereafter to be referred to as the POWs. . . . Saturday night we had a meeting with over 3,000 attending. That day there were sixty decisions. We could have had hundreds raise their hands but they prefer to hand-pick

the fruit through personal work by the hundreds of North Korean Christians who are among the POWs. Then Sunday at 6 AM we went to one of the larger enclosures. I am not permitted to indicate the number of POWs in the camp, but there were actually 9,000 at least who were present at that hour for prayer meeting. I'll never forget hearing them sing, "What can wash away my sin? Nothing but the blood of Jesus." For a solid hour the meeting lasted, just singing and prayer. Then I preached to a packed chapel for the GIs, and 3 officers and 21 men responded in the morning worship hour to the invitation for salvation, something unheard of there. Oh, how my soul magnifies the Lord!

Danger and death were sickeningly near as my father wrote on Independence Day, 1953.

A little while ago, I was with one of our heavy artillery units at the front. While I held my ears at the awful sound, their huge shells rocketed over a nearby hill and in a few short minutes inflicted almost 200 casualties on the enemy. As our jeep jolted over the rough mountain terrain, just a little ahead of us, one of our trucks struck a mine and was destroyed. All day long we have had to pull off the road to let our ambulances pass, rushing our fresh wounded back to medical care. All this is going on even as the radio reports peace and cease-fire negotiations are being talked about! In the midst of all this, however, I had a wonderful time of blessing and fellowship with Chaplain

Stemple, a true man of God. And everywhere there are invitations to preach. Many of these front-line troops haven't had a church service for weeks, and in every little meeting there are two or three who decide for Christ.

As always, the compelling needs of orphaned children weighed on Daddy's heart.

It rained all night last night and most of the morning, so instead of going to the front we drove down to Inchon, where the orphanage was which appeared in *38th Parallel.* I recognized three of the little kids who were there three years ago. The orphanage is running now, and little kids pouring in—picked up and sent there by GIs and chaplains. So we had a wonderful time. Gave them all balloons and then made arrangements to give them funds for two buildings to sleep in— desperately needed.

I also began arrangements through Chaplain Stemple to provide some sports equipment for them, as they had nothing to play with. The only heartache was to look for some of the darling faces I remember and to find them missing.

9 AT HOME WITH DADDY

In the latter part of 1953, we moved to Southern California. As usual, Daddy was gone and Mother came down to spend a week house hunting. The first house the realtor showed her was a lovely ranch-style home in Arcadia. As they pulled in the circle driveway, the realtor quickly explained that she knew it was much more than my folks could afford, but it was so lovely that she wanted Mom to see it.

Mother fell in love with it the moment she stepped through the door, but after a tantalizing tour she walked out, prudently pronouncing it completely out of the question.

By the end of the week, Mother had looked at a dozen houses and had seen nothing that could even begin to compare with the memory of that first house. Daddy flew in to see what she had found. Papa Johnson, who was living in nearby Altadena, drove Mother to the airport to pick him up.

"Well, what'd ya find?" Daddy inquired with his typical "Let's-get-on-with-it" air.

Before Mama could speak, Papa answered, "She found a house she really likes, but it's a bit expensive."

"Let's take a look at it."

The moment they drove into the driveway, Daddy squeezed Mother's hand and announced, "I like it!"

He walked from room to room knocking on walls, peeking into closets, and making all the appropriate "prospective buyer" sounds. But Mother could tell he was just going through the motions; he wanted the house. They all knelt then and there on the hardwood floor to commit the house to the Lord and to ask that if it was His pleasure for them to have it, He would provide a way. Then they called the realtor.

"Oh, I'm sorry," the realtor said. "I just finished typing up the escrow papers. The house is sold."

With a mixture of relief and disappointment, my folks went back to Portland, trusting the Lord that in His time He would give them a house.

A few weeks later the phone rang.

"Honey, I've got good news!" It was Papa calling from California. "The most amazing thing happened. I was in the market today when this woman stopped me and said, 'Aren't you Mr. Johnson?' It was your real-estate lady. How she ever remembered me I don't know, but she said the escrow fell through on the house and she's been desperate to reach you. If you want it, it's yours!"

And so God gave us our house on Santa Margarita Drive. It was a much lovelier house than Mother had ever dreamed of having. In fact, for the first few months she battled feelings of guilt that robbed her of joy in her new home.

Then one day she was talking with a friend, explaining her feelings. When she finished her friend said, "Lorraine, how do you receive a gift?"

"Why, I simply take it."

"Then what do you do?"

"I say 'Thank you.'"

"Don't you see that all God wants you to do is receive His gift and say thank you?"

It was a simple truth, but it released Mother to receive.

That very day she walked from room to room, laying hands on every wall and window, praising God and committing every square foot of the house to His honor and glory.

While Daddy was away, life was as relaxed and mellow as the Robert Goulet records Mama played as background music for her daydreams of Daddy's return. Our home was quiet and comfortable, the large, sunny rooms extending a gracious welcome to all who walked through the door. My mother's Swedish coffeepot always stood hot and full on the stove, filling the kitchen with an irresistible aroma.

I seldom remember coming home to an empty house. Mama was always waiting, her cheerful greeting assuring my childish heart that all was well. Although there was usually no one there to feed her feminine ego, she was always immaculately groomed, taking pride in her appearance for her own sake. And she taught us to do the same.

Although most of the time we were a group of women alone in a big house, I seldom remember being frightened or nervous. I knew the house belonged to Jesus; each night we prayed for the angels to "encamp around about us." Many nights as a small child I fell peacefully asleep, envisioning heavenly beings linked wing to wing surrounding our home.

Mother worked hard to give us a sense of family unity and tradition. We might all go our separate ways during the day (with one girl in high school, one in elementary school, and, later, one in diapers, there was little common ground during many of those years), but every evening the table was set with a brightly embroidered Korean cloth and we all sat down to eat by candlelight.

In 1956, when Daddy started his nationwide Sunday radio broadcasts, we'd arrange to sit down to Sunday dinner just as the World Vision quartet would sing "Send the Light," and we'd hear Daddy's friendly greeting, "Hi, neighbor!" It was nice, sort of like having him at the table with us and we looked forward to those half-hour visits. They made Daddy seem closer, and also helped keep us abreast of what he was doing!

From the moment we would get word that Daddy was flying in, the excitement would begin to mount. I could sense it in Mother's frequent laughter and her quickened step. Furniture that was usually only dusted was polished to a high sheen. The shag carpet, which had just been vacuumed, now was raked as well (and heaven help the first little foot to leave a print in the middle of that perfectly combed rug). With a good pair of gym socks you could slide the whole length of the kitchen on the high-glossed floor. The house smelled of lemon polish and fresh-cut roses, and it buzzed with anticipation.

Finally, we'd all pile into the car to make the familiar drive to Los Angeles International Airport.

I have no idea how many times through the years we stood at an airport gate, searching the travel-weary faces of passengers for the one we longed to see. But the first glimpse of my father's slightly rumpled figure never failed to put a lump in my throat and tears in my eyes. With cries of "Daddy" and "Sweetheart," we'd all attempt to rush into one pair of open arms, hugging and kissing and talking all at once. In some ways it was as if the lights were suddenly turned on, the cameras started rolling, and someone shouted "Action."

Daddy was home.

Inevitably, we'd celebrate Daddy's homecoming by stopping at some nice restaurant on the way home.

It didn't matter if it was morning, afternoon, or night—we'd just eat whatever seemed appropriate. After all, what's a celebration without food?

My family never ate a meal that wasn't blessed. At home, in a restaurant, on the beach—we always joined in prayer before we ate. When Daddy was home he usually said grace, and just as he rarely preached for less than an hour, so his prayers were of proportionate longevity. One thought would lead to another, and by the time he was through it seemed we had prayed around the world, country by country!

Eventually I learned to appreciate my father's table prayers. When I was eleven or twelve, a group of wonderful Korean pastors came to visit us. We all went out to dinner, and because there were twelve or fourteen of us, several tables were pushed together to form a long banquet table down the center of the dining room. This was one of those places where the lights are kept at a warm glow, dishes noiselessly appear and disappear, and the patrons sit quietly conversing in plush, cushioned booths.

When it came time to pray, Daddy asked one of our guests to do the honor. With tremendous dignity and pride the brother rose, closed his eyes, and proceeded to pray in Korean in a loud, healthy voice. When he sat down five minutes later, the entire room hung suspended in silence. No one even chewed. After that, I decided Daddy's prayers weren't so bad.

I realize now that Daddy was never home long enough to truly unwind. He was like a football player after a big game, exhausted but much too keyed up to relax. After a twenty-four-hour snooze, he'd be up and rarin' to go, determined to make up for lost time with trips to Disneyland and Knott's Berry Farm and nice restaurants. My younger sister Robin and I loved it. It was like Christmas, and Daddy was our own special Santa.

Of course, there was also work to be done while he was home. His correspondence alone was enough to keep someone busy full time. Then there were speaking engagements, the radio broadcasts, television interviews, and usually a film in the making. And there were always people dropping by—friends visiting from out-of-state or missionaries home on furlough.

One evening in the early sixties, Billy Graham came for dinner. During the evening's conversation he said, "Don't live so close to your office, Bob. Make your home someplace apart and away, so that when you're home you're really home. Otherwise, you'll never have a real home life."

At the time his advice made no great impression on any of us. But in years to come Mother would remember it and wonder if things might have been different had they taken it more seriously.

Some things stand out sharply in my memories of my dad. One time he brought home several large crates filled with minute, intricate pieces of wire and metal. Single-handedly, he was going to transform this assortment into the best stereo system this side of Tokyo. To Mother's chagrin, he carefully laid the pieces out over two-thirds of the living room floor. Only then did he discover that the instructions were in Japanese.

Surrounded by a sea of nuts and bolts, Daddy spent the rest of the day and much of the night attempting to decipher the diagrams. Finally he admitted defeat, piling the whole mess in one corner of the room until someone could be hired to put it together.

Our family loved games, especially word games, and the competition was tough. Both Mother and Sharon worked crossword puzzles to keep in shape, and we all read voraciously. Language was one of Daddy's major tools, and his vocabulary was impressive. But occasionally he'd slip one in like "hyquinox."

"Hyquinox!" we'd all scream in unison. "What's that?"

"Why, a hyquinox is a small brown seahorse-like creature found in the China sea, which is dried and ground into fine powder as seasoning for some of the most exotic Mandarin dishes," he'd reply without blinking an eye.

Dragging out our two-volume dictionary, one of us would confirm our suspicions—there was no such word. Dismissing our objections with a wave of his hand, Daddy would say, "That's not a comprehensive dictionary. There are lots of legitimate words that aren't included in that dictionary. And 'hyquinox' is one of them!"

Although there was much excitement and joy when Daddy was home, there was also an awkward sense that he was just visiting. Most of those years he never even bothered to unpack his suitcase, leaving it open and ready to go at a moment's notice. This was a real sore spot with my mom, who hated living with the constant reminder that her man was home only temporarily.

With Daddy gone so much, it was inevitable that we would fall into our own routines and habits. Mother was used to making decisions and exercising a certain amount of independence while Daddy was gone. We children became dependent upon her for some of the things we might naturally have looked to our father for if he had been there. Then Daddy would arrive. He was accustomed to being the person in authority, since he lived in a world where he was revered and treated with an awe peculiar to the famous and powerful. When he spoke, people listened. When he wanted something done, it was done. When he saw something he didn't like, it was changed.

After the first few days of homecoming, little conflicts would inevitably erupt. It was impossible not to step on one another's toes as we jostled around in search of our rightful positions.

I could always tell when Daddy was getting ready to leave—that's when the arguments usually occurred.

Lying in bed at night, my ears would perk up at the first sound of angry words, my heart pounding with dread. I suppose my folks fought a lot, considering the amount of time they had together. But I think I understand why. The farther away you are from someone, the louder you must shout to be heard. And about some things, my parents were worlds apart.

Usually the fights had something to do with Daddy's leaving. Mother would ask, "Why do you have to go?" Sometimes there was an obvious answer that Mother couldn't refute. Other times the reasons seemed vague and difficult to understand. Daddy seemed to be going simply because he wanted to, and Mother would feel hurt and angry.

Then, in the midst of the furor I'd hear Daddy say, "I know, Sweetheart," or "Honey, you just don't understand."

Sweetheart. Honey. It was all right. They still loved each other. My whole body would relax, and I'd slip off to sleep, confident the angry words were no threat to my world.

10 THE EVANGELICAL SYNDROME

My fifth year will always stand out in my mind, for it was then that *The Mickey Mouse Club* first appeared on our television screen, catching up me as well as three-fourths of the rest of the under-age-ten population in its magical spell. For the next few years I lived in a world of Mickey Mouse ears and Mouseketeers; a world where one could climb aboard a flying elephant named Dumbo and be transported to any place in the world in a matter of seconds.

Daddy, however, insisted on a more conventional means of transportation as he prepared to meet a queen. He had been asked to come to Washington, D.C., to speak at an International Christian Leadership Conference (ICL), and then stop in Amsterdam on his way to India to report to the honorary international president of the ICL, Queen Wilhelmina, princess of the Netherlands and mother of Queen Juliana. Daddy wrote from Holland on February 7, 1955:

> Her royal highness requested me to come to the palace at 10 this morning. A lovely Cadillac came and took me to that delightful old palace. There this old dear Christian saint,

who was queen for 50 years, received me in her apartment and for an hour and fifteen minutes we visited alone. She herself served me coffee and cakes, and then pumped me with questions about the churches in the Orient. She is very alert, very charming, and treated me with the greatest imaginable courtesy. Our visit ended with a precious season of prayer.

Four years later, Mother traveled with Daddy to meet not only the queen mother, Wilhelmina, but also the reigning queen, Juliana. By this time Daddy was used to rubbing elbows with royalty, but for Mother it was a Cinderella experience.

In Amsterdam, Mom and Dad checked into a lovely hotel and were informed that their audience with the queen would be at two the next day. At the appointed time, the long, black palace limousine pulled up in front of their hotel. Its presence immediately drew a crowd of curious onlookers who were eager to see the honored passengers. Mama felt like saying, "Sorry, it's just us," as they were seated by the uniformed chauffeur.

As they drove leisurely through the countryside, Mama was struck by the clear, bright freshness. Everywhere there were flowers and greenery. The people seemed to take great pride in their country and displayed a friendly, joyful spirit.

That's good, Lorraine. Talk about the country, Mother thought. And don't forget to curtsy and call the queen, "Your Royal Highness" and the queen mother "Your Majesty" . . . or is it the other way around?

Daddy took Mother's hand. "How do you feel?" he asked. "Are you nervous?"

She thought a moment and replied, "No, I'm terribly excited, but I'm not nervous."

Finally the car drove past the massive gates and wound its way through the immaculate grounds. The front steps were strewn with thousands of flowers, and the chauffeur explained that it is customary for the people to bring flowers on the queen's birthday, which had been the day before.

They were greeted at the steps by a gentleman who led them inside and through a maze of large and exquisitely furnished rooms. Finally they entered a small garden room. There, in this cozy, intimate setting, sat Queen Juliana and Queen Wilhelmina. All need for pomp and circumstance was immediately dismissed as they warmly greeted my folks and asked them to sit down.

The next thirty minutes raced by. Both ladies were extremely interested in Daddy's work, and they asked him many questions. Mother sat quietly, content to listen.

Then, to Mother's surprise, Queen Juliana turned to her and began conversing, as she poured tea from a lovely silver tea set and served pieces of her birthday cake. At first Mother found herself repeating her carefully rehearsed comments about the countryside, but soon the queen's natural friendliness put her at ease and she found herself talking much as she would with a dear friend. Both women had three daughters, and their motherhood gave them a whole world of common ground.

When Daddy saw that their time was up, he asked, "Would you mind if I pray with you before we go?"

"Not at all," came the reply. Mother was a bit startled to see Daddy kneel on the floor between the two queens. With a hand on each chair, he raised his head to heaven and prayed. *Who else but Bob would dare to do that and have two queens accept it as nothing unusual?* Mother thought.

The prayer over, they rose to go. Wilhelmina took Daddy's arm and walked him to the door.

But Juliana took Mother's hand and said, "Can I ask you something, Mrs. Pierce? How do you live alone without your husband? And how do you raise your children without their father?"

Mother's heart went out to her. She had read somewhere that there was trouble between the queen and her prince; the woman was definitely hurting.

Covering the queen's hand with her own, Mother said, "I can do it only because the Lord enables me to do it. And he does."

The two women talked for several more minutes. Mother was amazed at the words God gave her as the queen wept quietly.

In the car on the way back to the hotel, Daddy held Mama close and said, "I'm so proud of you, Sweetheart. You had a real ministry to the queen."

In September of 1955, Daddy held meetings in Seoul, Korea. He wrote:

> These last ten days have in some ways been my life's busiest. But how God has blessed! No doubt this conference, attended by 3,337 pastors besides others, has been the greatest thing of its kind in the Orient, if not elsewhere!

On the last day, more than 80,000 people climbed Namson Mountain to hear Daddy preach. The Korean army sent its band, and the university sent its orchestra. A choir of over 500 voices combined to sing praises to God for His transforming touch upon the Korean church during those days.

While Daddy was standing on a mountaintop ministering to 80,000 people, Mama was home washing my hair and reminding herself of 1 Samuel 30:24, which Papa Johnson often used to encourage her: "The share of the man who stayed with the supplies is to be the same as that of him who went down to the battle. All will share alike."

Although the scriptural reassurance of her significance in God's eyes was comforting, there were times when Mother couldn't help but express her loneliness and her desperate need for a closer relationship with Daddy.

I picture you eating lunch somewhere in Korea. It's 8 PM here. I've just finished shampooing Marilee's tresses, so thought I'd write at this advantageous time while she dries her hair. We are enjoying Daily Light together. I make Sharon read it every night at dinner. It's so nice to know, too, that you are reading it there. Every tie means so much to me. I can't seem to shake this terrible loneliness. I'm trying not to show it, though, and haven't mentioned it even to Dad.

We pray for you each day together, and I remember you several times a day. I don't want a moment of any day wasted. I pray to that end. If all these days are counted in God's great plan for souls and His kingdom's work, then I want to keep breathing, living, waiting for you.

Well, I don't mean to be morbid. If it bothers you, tear it up and don't read it again. But I told you I would be putting some things on paper that I'd been feeling for a long time. I have to. You do the same if you like. I want so badly for you to really know me—for me to know you. You seem so far from me at times and then again, you are so very much mine.

• • •

In 1956, Daddy brought twenty-six children from Korea to the arms of loving adoptive parents here in the States.

The job of single-handedly transporting twenty-six children halfway around the world was every bit as difficult as it sounds! Daddy wrote about the adventure:

> At the last minute, six children couldn't come because of the American embassy slip-up in mailing the necessary papers between Japan and headquarters in Korea. Then one child came down too sick to come. But we all got safely off. One little Negro baby had a fever and runny nose, but we all thought it was just a cold.
>
> After a five-hour flight we arrived in Tokyo, were 1 1/2 hours getting cleared, and then taken to a hotel to stay overnight. We were to leave at 6:15 PM on PAA the next evening, May 22. But about noon I called the doctor because two or three had fevers and the little black baby especially worried me. Well, the doctor took one look and said measles and that three others should go into the hospital for observation!
>
> Hospital after hospital turned us down on admittance, but thank God for the Catholics. They were as crowded as any, but have done everything! They aren't even supposed to take contagious cases, but stuck their necks out to help. They have our room sealed off and are taking excellent care of all six.
>
> And PAA is the most wonderful outfit in the world here. The head, Bill Ortwin, is an old friend of mine, and they got me nurses and Amahs (baby-tenders) who are with me around

the clock. I have one nurse and two Amahs at all times. But they don't speak English, and they open windows, allowing drafts on the fevered ones, and congregate in one room while little sick ones are left alone and terrified in the other. So I don't dare leave them at all. Of course, I am quarantined also, but I'm not sure for how long. And also, I really don't know if I've had measles, and if I have, they say you can have them again! So, fingers crossed!

Daddy's arrival home with those children was a big event. Newspaper and television newsmen were going to be there, and many of the prospective parents also would be meeting the plane. We also planned to be at the airport.

Now Mother has never functioned tremendously well at five in the morning, so to be sure we would not be late for the 7:00 AM flight arrival, we spent the night in an airport hotel. After instructing the desk to call us at six the next morning, we settled down for the night.

I was so excited I didn't think I would ever get to sleep. But the next thing I heard was Mother yelling hysterically into the phone, "It's 7:30! Why didn't you call us?"

Well, by the time we got there everything was over but the shouting—and I do mean shouting. Daddy was furious. No amount of explaining seemed to make a difference. All he knew was that he had just been through a week of nerve-racking, exhausting pandemonium and he had looked forward to stepping off the plane and seeing his family waiting—and we had failed him. No one had known where we were, and finally he had been left waiting with nothing to do but worry that something had happened to us.

Of course, no one was more upset about the mishap than Mother. She had the opportunity of sharing moments like that with Daddy so seldom that it was a real disappointment.

•   •   •

Never was Daddy's absence felt more keenly than on those special days families love to celebrate together. Birthdays. Anniversaries. Holidays. Daddy tried to be home on these days, but sometimes it just wasn't possible.

Thanksgiving, 1956, found Daddy in Beirut, Lebanon. We were all disappointed. It just wouldn't be Thanksgiving without Daddy there to carve the turkey. But, more importantly to my mother, it meant he would not be home to celebrate their twentieth anniversary. On November 24 he wrote from Istanbul:

> Twenty years ago today, tonight rather, we began together! My heart floods with memories of all the warm and good things we have had together. Remember our wedding night in Floyd's apartment? Remember the first

apartment by the Forum Theater? Remember the first little apartment in Glendale? Remember our "campaign" in Ojai? Remember the days in San Diego with Earl and Eunice Anderson and Brother Will South? Remember Palm Springs and Banning? Will you ever forget El Centro and the dingy room and air cooler? Most of all I remember you! You, and all these things, and a thousand other places and times. I loved you then, but I love you more now.

The year was 1957. Sharon was an independent sixteen-year-old, and I had just turned seven. For years Mother had stayed at home, fulfilling her obligation to her children. Her life had been an endless succession of hellos and goodbyes. Deep down inside, she believed Daddy's ceaseless wanderings would come to an end someday. Papa used to say, "Let him go, Honey. Eventually he's got to slow down."

But the years passed, and Daddy showed no signs of slowing down. The work kept growing, and he became a man in perpetual motion. In January and February of 1957, he visited the Philippines.

The opening night everything was packed out. One paper said 50,000. This is the largest thing of its kind Protestants have ever seen in the Philippines. And how I want to thank God for His goodness; 388 decisions the first night. Last night all seats were filled. The crowd was 9,000 to 10,000 and 245 definite, weeping sinners came forward. I praise God for His anointing and power.

The Maramon Convention in India:

Tonight is a great triumph for our Lord. I preached to 30,000 men, gave an altar call, and there was a wonderful response. Praise Him! This afternoon we dedicated a student center built by World Vision. These poverty-ridden students gave an offering of over $50 U.S. to build a fence around it. This represents several days' food for each of over a hundred students!

Assam:

The days in Assam were a thrill. They live in such primitive conditions, but the Christians were so radiant and so thrilled to have us come. And the Bible School, mud-floored, thatch-roofed, mud-walled, already has 100 students attending it.

Afghanistan:

Afghanistan is "out of this world," like the most remote, primitive parts of China. But Christie Wilson, our missionary, is doing an historic work. About 125 people came to the meeting the night I spoke. A doctor, Herbert MacKell from New York, was there also, and Christie said that the three of us ordained ministers were the largest group of preachers ever in Afghanistan at one time in modern centuries.

The U.S.S.R.:

I thought of you again and again. Especially when I thought that on arrival in Moscow they might have time to ascertain who I am and might have detained me. Funny feeling the whole time, believe me!

Then Daddy was on to Austria, Greece, Italy, and France. It became obvious that if Mother and Daddy were to have anything more than an occasional marriage, Mother would have to be the one to change. Now that we girls were old enough to do without her some of the time, she began to look forward to taking a more active part in Daddy's ministry.

God even provided the perfect babysitter. Grammy, my maternal grandmother, was now widowed and living close by. She and Mother had reconciled and become very close in the past years, and we girls adored her. Mother knew she could leave us with perfect peace in Grammy's care.

But there were other obstacles to overcome. While she considered herself fully recovered from her previous nervous breakdown, Mother would occasionally suffer an attack of nerves that would leave her physically and emotionally incapable of handling large crowds of people—a real problem, considering that a good portion of Daddy's life was spent dealing with the masses. But these attacks were few and far between, and physically Mother was feeling strong and optimistic.

She had had several close calls in planes, and she avoided them whenever possible. But she was determined not to let fear deprive her of being with her husband. So now, claiming Romans 8:39 as her very own, she prepared to see the world.

As a first step, she flew with Daddy to New York City for a Billy Graham crusade at Madison Square Garden. Everybody was there, and Mother loved seeing so many old friends and being a part of all the excitement. Mostly, she loved being with my dad. Everything would have been perfect if it hadn't been for an irritating touch of flu that kept her slightly nauseated all the time. She took some milk of magnesia and tried to ignore the discomfort.

After the Graham crusade, Daddy was to hold several meetings in Buffalo. But by the time they got there, Mother's flu had worsened, leaving her too sick at times to even get out of bed. Finally, Daddy decided she should go home.

Upon arrival in Los Angeles, Mother went immediately to her doctor. After a careful examination, he told her, "I'm afraid you have a tumor. I want you to see a specialist."

The specialist tested Mother thoroughly and then sat her down in his office. "Your doctor was right. You have a tumor. But you also have a baby."

On the way home her thoughts were spinning. All concern over the tumor was replaced by the thought of a baby. "I'm going to have a baby. At forty years of age! It just can't be! Why, Lord? Just when I was free to be with Bob some of the time. And oh! What will Bob say?"

But Daddy's response surprised Mother. "Finally, the Lord is going to bless me with a son!" he declared most confidently. Seeing that Daddy was pleased made all the difference to Mama, and she too began looking forward to the arrival of a boy child. In fact, as her body began to change and she felt the new life within her, she positively glowed.

This time there was money to buy all the things she never had with her first two pregnancies—clothes, furniture, and the perfect nursery, decorated in blue, of course. But the one thing Mama wanted most was for Daddy to slow down a bit and share the joy of those months with her. Her first pregnancies had been during difficult times; now she felt God was giving them a chance to redeem much of what they had missed before.

Daddy was torn. He loved Mother and truly looked forward to the arrival of this child. But he carried a great weight of responsibility, and he had been caught up long ago in what I have heard Dr. Jack Hayford describe as "the evangelical syndrome"—the misconception that a man can serve God to the fullest only if he is willing to put ministry before family. How many times I heard Daddy quote Luke 14:26, "If anyone comes to me and does not hate his father and mother, his wife and children . . . he cannot be my disciple." Daddy understood that Scripture to mean that he was obliged to put his ministry and the needs of the world before his own family. He used to say,

"I've made an agreement with God that I'll take care of His helpless little lambs overseas if He'll take care of mine at home."

It surely sounded sensible enough, and Daddy sincerely believed it was right. Unfortunately, future events would prove that this was Daddy's agreement, not God's.

11 KOREA WELCOMES MRS. BOB PIERCE

It would be presumptuous of me to judge what God required of Daddy and what Daddy required of himself. Surely God blessed my father's endeavors because they were done out of a heart that yearned to please him and see Jesus Christ exalted. And although Daddy would not seriously consider staying home, he wasn't insensitive to Mother's feelings. He did not consider her objections unreasonable; in his opinion they were merely impractical.

Such was the case in the latter months of 1957. World Vision had scheduled a series of pastors' conferences throughout the Orient, after which Daddy was to hold a crusade in Seoul. He could see no way to alter his schedule, even though the baby's birth was only three months away.

Fortunately he was home from the crusade in time to check Mother into St. Luke's Hospital on December 21. Her contractions were strong and regular, but it became obvious that the labor could go on for a while.

Partially sedated, it was all Mama could do to keep on top of the pain when she heard Daddy slap the doctor on the back and say, "Come on, Doc. Let's get this show on the road!" A few minutes later labor was induced, and within the hour Mother was wheeled into the delivery room. A few strong pushes later the child emerged, arms flailing and announcing to the world with a loud, healthy cry that it had arrived.

"Congratulations, you have a beautiful baby girl," the doctor announced. And she was beautiful—chubby and pink, her head a mass of dark, curly hair.

"Oh, Lord, don't let Bob be too disappointed," Mama prayed as she drifted off to sleep.

Sometime later Mama awoke in her room. It was the middle of the night, but Daddy was by her bed, tenderly leaning over her and stroking her hair. "Just wanted you to know," he whispered, "she's the most beautiful baby in the nursery." They named her Robin after her daddy ("Robin" is "Robert" in Scottish).

A few months later, after another overseas trip, Daddy reported the reaction on the mission field to Robin's birth. Many had been praying for and awaiting with great anticipation the arrival of Dr. Pierce's son. For them, the news of a third daughter was quite a disappointment. "They said we weren't to worry, though," Daddy told his forty-one year old wife with a grin. "The next child will surely be a boy!"

•   •   •

The year 1960 marked the tenth anniversary of World Vision's involvement in Korea, and Daddy was to receive the highest honor that country bestows on a foreigner. Immediately following, he was to go to Osaka, Japan, for a city-wide crusade. It was the perfect time for Mother to make her first trip to the Orient.

Stepping off the plane was like stepping into another world. There to greet them was a great crowd of people, with a huge banner—"Welcome Dr. and Mrs. Bob Pierce"—held high over their heads. Supervisors and missionaries from all over the country had been flown in for this special occasion. And there were children—dozens of beautiful, eager-faced boys and girls dressed in traditional Korean garb. As Mother and Dad approached, one after another shyly came forward, bowing as they presented their gifts of flower leis.

After endless bowing and hand-shaking, Mother and Dad climbed into a jeep with Erv and Flo Raetz and Marlin and Kay Nelson, World Vision's directors in Korea, and they jolted along the dusty, pock-marked road into Seoul.

Arriving at the World Vision House, Mrs. Raetz led the way to the Pierce Room, a cheerful, immaculate room that had been Daddy's home away from home for years. The bed was covered with a beautiful, handmade quilt; the fireplace was laid and awaited a match.

Mother looked forward to a shower and a change of clothes after the long flight, but no sooner had she set her bag down when Daddy announced, "We've got to get going. They're expecting us at one of the children's homes, and we mustn't be late!" And that was the way it was for the next ten days—much to see and little time to see it.

The thrill of seeing that first children's home was overwhelming. As they pulled up, the superintendents and the little ones were lined up out front, waiting to greet them with a lively chorus of "Jesus Loves Me." When the song was over, the children surrounded my folks, grabbing a handful of skirt or coat and raising their little arms to be picked up. They were starved for affection, and they wanted to be touched and held. Mother bent down to pick one up.

"Honey, don't pick up even one," Daddy warned. "If you hold one, you'll have to hold them all and we'll be here all day." It was heartbreakingly hard to ignore their outstretched arms, but Mother knew he was right.

The next day they went to an infant home, where newborns and small babies lay in row upon row of neatly kept cribs. Mother took one look, and her eyes filled with tears. They were so little, so innocent, so helpless. She looked at Daddy.

"Go ahead. These you can pick up," Daddy said as he settled back to wait as Mother went from bed to bed, tenderly cuddling each little one.

As they walked into the next room, they were met with a pitiful sight. This room was filled with less fortunate children—many were weak and sick from months of starvation endured before their arrival at the home. One little boy was particularly pathetic;

his baby arms and legs were little more than skin and bones, and his little body was twisted and crippled. Mother wanted to give him a comforting hug, but she was stopped. "I'm sorry, Mrs. Pierce," a nurse quickly explained. "You'd better not. He's terribly weak. You see, although he looks no more than two, this little boy is six years old."

"Oh, Jesus!" Mother prayed, as she wept over that precious little life. No wonder Daddy hadn't been able to walk away. All the years of sacrifice took on a new significance as she saw for herself the good they had accomplished.

After the tour was over, the missionaries who ran the Children's Center asked Mother and Dad to lunch. Entering their home, Mother was again impressed, as she had been at the World Vision House, with how wonderfully these missionary wives succeeded in establishing their own sense of gracious living and tradition in their homes. The table was beautifully set and laden with cheeses, cold meats, little cakes, and luscious cookies—a real feast, topped off with strong, hot cups of freshly ground coffee, an unexpected treat in this land of tea.

Afterward, Mother couldn't help commenting on how well the missionaries ate. "Oh, they don't eat like that every day," Daddy laughed, shaking his head. "They've known for months that you were coming, and all those cookies and cakes were sent in tins as Christmas presents from their families. That coffee is especially dear, as they only get a pound a year. They saved it all these months to serve to you as an expression of their love."

All during Mother's stay, there were many such loving expressions by the selfless and giving missionaries of Korea. Mother was all the more glad she had brought a little surprise for them. Aware that there was rarely money to spend on new clothes, she had brought a dozen stylish new dresses in assorted colors and sizes. For years afterward, she received letters from these missionary wives mentioning how much those dresses meant.

One Sunday Mother and Dad attended Young Nak Church, which at that time was the largest Presbyterian church in the world. During the service, Mother was asked to say a few words of greeting. It was the first time she spoke through an interpreter, and she did her best to express her great joy at finally being there after all those years. As she finished her short speech, she noticed that most of the women were weeping profusely. Tears were streaming down their cheeks, and some were hiding their faces in handkerchiefs to keep from sobbing out loud.

"What did I say?" she asked. "Did I say something wrong?"

"Not at all, Darling," Dad replied. "They're weeping with joy. They've waited ten long years to see you."

On the day Daddy was presented the Medal for Public Welfare Service in "recognition of his exceptionally praiseworthy service to the Republic of Korea," Mother accompanied him to the palace in Seoul and stood proudly at his side while President Syngman Rhee made the presentation. It was a fitting and wonderful way to end her first visit to Korea.

Before they left for Japan, Mother and Daddy visited the World Vision office to say good-bye. Erv and Flo Raetz took Mother into their office and handed her a plain white envelope. Inside was a note that said, "Dear Mrs. Pierce, We are so happy that you have come, we would like to pay your way." It was signed, "The Superintendents." Accompanying the note was a check for one thousand dollars, every penny given out of their meager salaries and their abundance of love.

12 THE GATHERING STORM

For months, Christian businessmen and pastors had worked together to prepare the way for the Osaka crusade. Daddy was coming to do what had never been done in Japanese history—to hold three weeks of evangelistic meetings in the beautiful new convention center.

The sight was overwhelming as Mother and Daddy stepped off the plane. People were everywhere, crowding against the restraining arms of officials who were instructed to allow only the press on the field. The security was so tight that even World Vision staff were not allowed through. In desperation, Larry Ward (then editor of *World Vision* magazine, later the founder of Food for the Hungry) went up to a guard and flashed a gasoline credit card, hoping he couldn't read English and would assume it was a press card. And so it was that the first thing Mama and Daddy saw was Larry's smiling face waiting at the bottom of the steps to help guide them through the throng and into a large black limousine, the first of a twenty-car procession that leisurely wound its way from the airport into the city of Osaka.

Arriving at the hotel, they were once again met by an army of reporters and flashing cameras. Daddy was placed on a small platform, and it was announced that a great man of God had come to that city.

Mother has described the Osaka crusade as one of the greatest thrills of her life. Every day the people would line up hours ahead of time, filling the large convention hall to capacity. The majority were students and young people, and although some missionaries considered them the hardest to reach, they were irresistibly drawn by the Spirit of God.

Each evening Ralph Carmichael conducted the Osaka Symphony Orchestra and a three-hundred-voice choir in a soul-stirring program of old hymns and contemporary Christian music. Then Daddy would stand up, his beloved interpreter Mr. Kita by his side, and present the simple message of the gospel. When the message ended, Daddy would give the altar call. First there would be a hesitation; then, as if in response to some heavenly signal, people would begin to rise—men and women, the young, the old, students, businessmen, housewives—an irrepressible wave of people would fill up the front of the auditorium and overflow halfway up each aisle.

During the day, Mother was usually left to herself, as Daddy was kept busy from early morning until after the services. But one night no service was planned, and Mother and Daddy decided to get away alone for twenty-four hours. They and a couple of World Vision men boarded an express train for Kyoto, one of the most beautiful and historic cities in Japan.

Arriving in Kyoto at midnight, they drove through the quiet darkness to a beautiful Japanese inn, nestled among trees and spotlighted by an enormous full moon. Pointing to the moon, Daddy gave Mom a hug and whispered, "Special order, just for you." The inn was Japanese style, designed to cater to rich Japanese, not to the tourist trade. Upon entering their room, Mother saw their beds were *tatamis,* straw-like mats on the floor accompanied by thick, quilted comforters. The tables and mirror were all close to the floor, and not a chair was in sight.

After settling their things in their room, the World Vision men picked them up and took them to a geisha house. Traditionally, women are not allowed in geisha houses, but this had been specially arranged for Mother. They were greeted by several beautiful girls and were seated in a private room and served tea while the geishas danced and played instruments.

A little later, several of the girls gathered around her, talking and giggling. "They're fascinated by your blond hair," one of the men explained. "They'd like to touch it, if you don't mind." And so the East touched the West.

After an hour or so, the men took Mother back to the room. "You haven't really experienced Japan until you take a bath Japanese style," they explained to Mother. They told her the custom included the help of a geisha girl if you are a man, or a geisha boy if you are a woman.

Petrified, Mother entered the bathroom, reassuring herself that if it was the custom and if Daddy was doing it, it must be proper. Relieved to find she was alone, she looked at the large, high-walled wooden vat of steaming water. "If I can get in before the geisha boy comes, I'll be all right," she thought to herself. "But how do I get in? The walls are so high."

Just then she spotted a small wooden stool. She had just stepped up on it when she heard the door opening. She froze. Her towel was on a bench halfway across the room.

"*Combowa*. I am your geisha boy," Daddy said in his funny pidgin English, bursting with laughter at the look on Mother's face. He explained that the whole thing was a joke the boys had thought up. Then he asked, "Woman, what are you doing?"

"I was just trying to get in the tub."

"You don't get in the water. That stool is to sit on. You suds yourself up and then use that pan over there to scoop water out and rinse yourself off. That bath water is for the entire inn!" he exclaimed as he began lathering her back.

The crusade in Osaka ended, and Mother and Dad prepared to fly home. Their farewell was even greater than their welcome, for the whole city had been touched by the hand of God during those three weeks. The papers had been full of glowing reports. The churches had experienced revival and an explosive increase in attendance.

But mostly it was the young people who had so wholeheartedly responded to the message of salvation. Passing through the hotel lobby on their way to the train station, Mother and Daddy were mobbed by an enormous crowd of weeping, eager students, pressing in to say goodbye, arms reaching out from all directions just to touch my folks as they passed.

At the station they were greeted by more than a thousand people waiting to see them off. Once again a path had to be cut through the forest of bodies. Mother and Daddy smiled and touched as many as they could while still walking ahead.

Finally they boarded the train, standing at a window as the train pulled out. One girl who was close to the window slipped off her class ring and held it out to Mother. Mama couldn't understand what she was saying, but she could tell by her face that she wanted her to have it. As she took the ring, Mama felt tears rolling down her own cheeks as the young girl's face lit up in a glowing smile. "Thank you," she said in halting English. "Thank you!"

• • •

The next year a crusade was scheduled in Tokyo. After the thrill of Osaka, Mother looked forward to returning to Japan. Many churches had extended invitations for her to minister to the women.

Mother and Daddy decided to go by ship, joining Paul and Edith Rees for the two-week voyage. The trip promised to be pleasant and restful. Mother had never met Edith Rees before, but the two hit it off immediately. The only thing Mother didn't like was being totally cut off from home for days at a time. Although she had total peace about leaving us with Grammy, it would have been comforting to know that in case of an emergency she could pick up a phone or jump on a plane and be home in hours.

After five days at sea the ship docked in Hawaii, and Mother called home. Grammy reassured her that all was well, and Mother began the twelve-day voyage between Hawaii and Yokohama with only minor trepidation. After a few days she and Daddy both began to really relax, enjoying the lazy, leisurely days away from the pressures that had become a way of life.

One morning Mother was sitting at her dressing table, thinking how glad she was she had come. She and Daddy were getting along famously, she really liked the Reeses, and after this refreshing break they had another Osaka experience to look forward to. She hummed as she brushed her hair, realizing with a smile that she was singing one of Grammy's favorite hymns, "God answers prayer in the morning, God answers prayer at noon, God answers prayer in the evening, so keep your heart in tune."

The door opened and Daddy walked in. "Good morning, Sweetheart," Mother cheerfully greeted him. "Be ready in a minute."

"Lorraine." The way he spoke her name caused her heart to sink as she turned to look at him.

"Lorraine, I'm going to tell you the way I'd want to be told if it were my mother. Your mother's gone. She died this morning."

Faced with seven more days at sea, Mother did her best to carry on, dressing for dinner each night but spending most of her time in her room, overwhelmed by an unendurable sense of loss and pain. After a couple of days she could stand it no longer.

"Please, Bob. I've got to know what's happening at home. I don't know who has the children or when Mother's being buried. I don't even know how she died!"

Daddy went to the wireless room to try to send a message. "Sorry, sir," he was informed. "We're heading into a typhoon and already have received a couple of SOSs. We have to keep our set clear to receive emergency calls."

And so the ship braved the typhoon. At one point the waves battered the ship so fiercely that the porthole in my parents' cabin was blown out. As Mother watched in astonishment, water poured in through the gaping hole, soaking the carpet and beds. Their things would have been ruined if Daddy and several stewards hadn't rushed in to transfer everything to a dry room.

But even the fury of the storm didn't really bother Mother. Numb with the pain of loss, she was far less concerned than poor Edith, who had no such emotional anesthetic to ease her fears. Nevertheless, every morning Edith would knock at Mother's door, bringing hot coffee and a cheerful word to help her face the day. For the remainder of the trip, Edith was her constant companion. During those emotional hours, the foundation of a lifelong friendship was laid.

Finally docking in Yokohama, Mother and Dad discussed what they should do. Daddy offered to fly home immediately to conduct the funeral. He felt Mother should stay, since we girls were well taken care of and there was nothing she could do. And Grammy had wanted her to come on this trip.

So Mother stayed in Tokyo while Daddy flew the many hours home, settled things there, then made the weary trip back to open the crusade.

Within two years of Grammy's homegoing, both Papa and Grandma Pierce also went to be with the Lord. All three had been powerful prayer warriors on my parents' behalf—praying through the various crises, supporting the ministry, and generally providing a consistent covering of prayer. Once those prayers were silenced, all hell broke loose.

•   •   •

A play-by-play description of the disintegration of a life or a family is neither easy to write nor easy to read. Certainly it was a nightmare to live.

Years of eighteen-hour days, sleep caught on planes, unsanitary food, and eternal jet lag had begun to take their toll on my father. Not only did he begin to experience a constant string of physical difficulties and exhaustion, but his emotional reserves were depleted. The temper that he had battled all his life to control got the upper hand more and more often, and the mind that had once operated with computer-like accuracy began short-circuiting, resulting in increasingly erratic behavior.

Others had stood by for years shaking their heads and making ominous predictions to one another on the inevitable outcome if Daddy didn't slow down, but they were too intimidated by his position and his ministry to deal with him directly about it.

If only my father had learned in the early years to say no occasionally, or perhaps to delegate more responsibility instead of trying to carry the full backbreaking load himself. How often I heard Daddy say, "Just let me burn out for God." But we are to be the light of this world, and a candle that burns out sheds no light. As surely as I know my father's ministry was ordained of God for his honor and glory, I know the following events grieved the Father's heart and were not in keeping with his will for my family.

The first rumblings of the coming storms were heard in 1963. Daddy had come home and had gone directly into St. Luke's Hospital for a series of tests. He needed a cure for a body that was beginning to fall apart piece by piece.

He left the hospital just in time to attend a World Vision board meeting, totally unprepared for what was coming. The board voted to cancel World Vision's weekly radio broadcasts.

Daddy's broadcasts had been airing for seven years. Next to his travels overseas, they were his most cherished extension of ministry. The radio was his direct line to the people—his pulpit. He foresaw his broadcasts as a stepping stone to a television program that would bring a missionary challenge into thousands of homes every week.

Daddy felt betrayed, not only because he'd lost something very dear, but because he had honestly expressed his desire to stay on the air and still had been overruled. For the first time his authority and control had been challenged, and the experience left him shaken and deeply wounded. Seeds of suspicion and bitterness had been planted, and Mother watched anxiously as he began to walk an emotional tightrope.

Toward the end of that year, Daddy was overseas and we were preparing for the holidays when Mother received a letter saying he had decided not to come home. He was ill and in need of complete rest, and he had decided to spend some time in seclusion.

Sick with concern and dissatisfied with the sketchy explanation, Mother found a friend willing to lend her the money to join him. But Daddy refused to let her come. Rejecting her offer of comfort and help, he chose to go it alone. World Vision put him on medical leave, and Dick Halverson became the acting president.

Daddy rarely wrote during the next nine months, and he talked very little about them afterwards, but a letter he wrote in May gave us some insight into the painful sense of isolation and confusion he was battling.

> I love you. . . . With all my heart. . . . More than life. In the stormy seas through which I have sailed alone since Christmas the visibility has been so low I have been unable to see my way, much less announce it. And I cannot see ahead now. But you have not been one moment out of my heart and mind. I know that you are cared for, and recent months have revealed you will therefore not miss me too much.

While Daddy was gone, Mother carried on as normally as possible. Most of the time she had no idea where or how Daddy was, so once again the only way to touch him was with arms of prayer.

For the family, those months were shaded by a hazy covering of fear, like a thin layer of smoke curling around the edges of our consciousness, giving everything an unnatural tint.

In the summer of 1964, World Vision held a conference at Winona Lake, Indiana. With Daddy gone, Mother had no desire to go. She dreaded the inevitable questions for which she had no answers, and she felt totally incapable of displaying confidence and optimism. But Daddy's absence made her presence all the more essential, and so she prepared to fulfill her obligation as "first lady."

Two images stick in my mind from that week in Indiana. One is of my mother standing in a reception line next to Dick Halverson at the president's reception, shaking an endless succession of outstretched hands, greeting many by name and all with a warmth that belied the great effort it took her.

The other is of a fourteen-year-old girl holding a telephone receiver to her ear and listening to her father's voice. World Vision had set up a booth where people could hear a prerecorded greeting from my dad, including his regret at not being there. I'll never forget the feeling in the pit of my stomach as I heard my father's voice for the first time in eight months. He sounded so close. I remember talking to his voice, telling him how much I loved him and wanted him home, then weeping uncontrollably because I knew he couldn't hear me.

Later, during a main service, a call was put through to my dad so he could speak directly to those gathered.

Then the phone was brought backstage and Mother, Robin, and I each had a chance to say hello. Afterward I felt confused and deeply saddened, realizing it had been easier to express my heart to the recording than to my father.

In October, Mother received a telegram from Daddy asking if he could come home for his fiftieth birthday. The fact that he asked permission shows the insecurity and alienation he was battling.

Once again the house was filled with that special buzz of anticipation as we prepared for the reunion. Daddy was coming home!

13 END OF AN ERA

The next few years passed with only occasional tremors. Daddy eased back into an active role with World Vision, concentrating his efforts on film projects like *The Least Ones* and *Viet Nam Profile,* slowly gaining momentum until he would resume his position as active president once again.

In 1965, when I was fifteen, I made my first and only trip to the Orient. Seeing the work firsthand made a tremendous impression on me, as it had on my mother. I felt my own heart break over the desperate need and despairing hopelessness of a world that was both familiar and alien to me. And, like my father, I was captivated by the mystical beauty of the Orient.

But I think the greatest benefit of that trip was seeing my dad in action. In the States he was well known and respected, but the Orient was full of people who had not only heard of World Vision, but who were *alive* because of it. My father was not just a celebrity there; he was a hero whom God had sent to touch their lives.

Nowhere are heroes treated with greater respect or honor than in Asia. The awe and reverence that constantly surrounded my dad was a revelation to me. Everywhere we turned there were people smiling and bowing, not only out of tradition, but out of their great love for my father. And the missionaries were no less demonstrative, taking precious time out of their busy schedules to be with my dad and to make me feel welcomed. We stayed in the finest hotels, where we were always greeted with the warmth accorded to highly preferred guests.

At airports we would often be met by airline officials who would stamp our passports and whisk us through customs before most of the other passengers were even off the plane.

I had known since I was very young that my father was different from the average dad. I remember the first time someone was impressed by my parentage. I was in first or second grade, making the monotonous bus journey to school with the same kids I rode with every day. I found myself talking to a girl I didn't know very well. Somehow, the subject of our dads came up.

"What's your dad do?" she asked.

"Oh, he just travels a lot and preaches. He's president of World Vision," I answered.

"World Vision! Is your dad Bob Pierce? We listen to him on the radio every Sunday, and I have two 'brothers' in Korea! Hey," she yelled, excitedly poking another kid in the side, "Did you know that Marilee is Bob Pierce's daughter!"

I don't remember anyone else getting particularly excited by her announcement, but I was deeply impressed with her extraordinary behavior. After that, I would occasionally find a way to casually mention my dad's name, throwing it out to see if it got any reaction.

It was fun being the daughter of someone famous. Of course, it would never do for me to appear impressed with the fact myself and often I would don a façade of false modesty. "Oh, you've probably never heard of him," I'd say, protecting myself from that embarrassing possibility. But as many times as not the name rang a bell, and it was a warm, special feeling to find myself illuminated by a corner of the spotlight in which my father lived.

Only later did that spotlight become a little annoying, as I attempted to establish my own identity rather than always being "Bob Pierce's daughter." I didn't battle any great resentment or feel anything but pride in being a Pierce, but more than once I remember teasing my dad with the threat, "Someday you're going to be introduced as 'Marilee Pierce's father,' and we'll see how you like it!"

I liken my dad, in those final years of his association with World Vision, to the last of the great dinosaurs—an endangered species struggling to survive in a changing world.

My father was a maverick, an innovator, a pioneer, and a visionary. The key to his whole ministry was his unhesitating responsiveness to need. If he saw a need that no one else was meeting, he met it. That's why World Vision was created—to organize and finance the fulfillment of the commitments my father made. While they were small, the supply and demand balanced out, although not without God's miraculous intervention time and again. But that was what made the ministry so exciting and satisfying.

But as World Vision expanded, the projects became larger and the sums of money grew astronomically. Millions of dollars passed through the office each year, and every penny had to be scrupulously accounted for. The government required detailed expense accounts, and of necessity the World Vision board began placing certain restrictions on Daddy's authority to commit money without their voted approval.

He did his best to comply, but my father was a free spirit, accustomed to checking only with the Holy Spirit before making on-the-spot commitments. For instance, in 1958 Daddy produced the film *A Cry in the Night*. It was tremendously moving, shot with care, creativity, and cinematic style. It also had the largest budget of any Christian film produced to date, a fact that raised a few eyebrows and made people particularly jumpy about getting the money back.

Just before the film was to be released, Daddy called everyone together and made the startling announcement that the Lord had told him to lend the film out for free. The only stipulation he made was that whoever asked for the film would pay the postal fees and take an offering for their own missions' projects.

No one could believe Daddy was serious, but at that time Daddy still had the final word. Within one year there were two hundred copies of *A Cry in the Night* working around the clock all over the country, and the increase in giving from people who saw the film was greater than from any other single project up to that time.

But Daddy's track record didn't make his unorthodox methods any easier to accept, and to the board he often appeared as impetuous as he had to Mother thirty years before when he had dropped their rent money into the passing offering plate. In all fairness, I know there were times when God used the board to keep Daddy from stretching things too thin. But the fact remains that Daddy often seemed to be on one end of a tug-of-war and the board on the other. Asking him now to function by a different set of rules meant a whole change in his approach to ministry, a change he resented and resisted. As a result, he and the board had a number of confrontations concerning unauthorized expenditures.

My father never handled confrontations well. Bill Price, my dad's personal assistant and constant companion for nearly eight years, said recently, "Your father's single greatest flaw was his explosive temper. But other than that—his morality, his vision, his dedication, his faith—for all these things I don't know any other man I respect as much as Dr. Bob. Countless times I watched him reach out, heedless of his own personal safety, to embrace the untouchable, the unlovely.

"I remember so clearly our last trip together. We were visiting a hospital in Formosa when Dr. Bob spotted a ten-year-old boy with meningitis. There was nothing more they could do for him, and he was lying in the corridor waiting to die. He watched us approach with large, frightened eyes, too weak to raise his head or wipe away the tears that slowly rolled down his cheeks. Dr. Bob stopped and, without a thought as to how highly contagious the disease was, wrapped the boy in his arms and prayed with him. I watched the child's body relax as Dr. Bob held him, and we left him peacefully at rest in the Savior's tender care.

"It was such a paradox to see the same man who gave so lovingly explode over the most unexpected things."

Daddy's unpredictable moods had always caused us to step lightly; we were never certain what might set him off. So it was with a deep sense of dread and fear that Mother watched Daddy walk out the door one day in 1967. Once again he and the board had butted heads over several issues, and the day promised fireworks of the most spectacular kind.

Daddy had talked while he dressed. "I'm going in and tell them this is the way I operate . . . the way God has blessed me . . . the only way I know to work. They knew that when they signed on. I haven't changed. I can't face a hungry, dying world and tell them to wait while I go home and check with my board. There is no way I can come home and get board approval for every little thing!"

Mother had heard everything Daddy was saying countless times before, and so had the board. But there was something different about this time. With sudden clarity, Mother realized that Daddy shouldn't be facing those men that day. He needed physical rest and emotional refreshing, a time to get alone with the Lord and be spiritually refueled. At the moment he was flying on empty, and any strong winds of opposition could cause him to lose control.

"I'm going to tell them to either pull with me or get off the ship!" he declared as he slammed the door behind him.

The next hours crawled past. The meeting went well past its scheduled duration, each additional minute adding to Mother's foreboding that something was wrong. Finally, late in the afternoon, Mama heard Daddy's car pull into the driveway. She rushed to open the door.

"Well, I let them have it all," he said in a tense, unnatural voice that slapped the air with each word.

"What do you mean?" Mother asked. "What are you talking about?"

"I gave them everything—my films, my office, my work. I told them if they wanted it so badly they could have it. I started with nothing; I'll leave with nothing!" As he spoke, his voice trembled with rage. There was no room for discussion or thoughtful reevaluation of the situation. Mother desperately tried to make him see what he was doing, but he was blind and deaf to anything but his own fury.

Mother rushed to the phone and called one of Daddy's most trusted friends, hoping his voice could call Daddy back to reason. For the moment, however, everyone was the enemy. Daddy told his friend to stay out of his business and hung up the phone.

The next day World Vision presented him with legal documents of agreement, and Bob Pierce signed his life's work away.

•   •   •

The next few months passed as if someone had died. Things continued in a seemingly normal pattern. We ate and drank and breathed and slept just as we always had, but everything was different. Life had taken a sudden and unexpectedly sharp turn, leaving us all painfully off balance. Suddenly there were no clear-cut definitions, because the thing that had controlled and defined the purpose of our existence—the ministry— was gone. Ten-year-old Robin spoke for us all the day she asked, "Who are we now, Mama?"

Jesus was still the foundation our lives were built upon, the solid Rock that is the same yesterday, today, and forever. But the support beams of that foundation had been the work God had given us. Everything had emanated from that—our friends, our family relationships, our attitude about ourselves. We lived in the quiet assurance that we belonged to something truly remarkable, something that exalted Jesus Christ and served mankind and gave our lives a special meaning and purpose. Now, suddenly, we were outside that warm, magical circle, no longer a part of the family that God had given birth to through us. It was crazy, impossible, ridiculous, and totally terrifying.

For Mother, the following year was a kaleidoscope of emotions. Her mind would rage with indignation when she thought of how Daddy had thrown away their life's work in a fit of temper, the way a petulant child might throw away a toy he can't work properly. Then, the anger would melt into teeth-grinding sorrow as reality flooded in, followed by incredulous disbelief that such a thing could happen.

During that time, Mother fought hard to hold on to the knowledge that God was still in control. Now the previous years of tenacious prayer and disciplined faith held her in good stead. She believed God because she knew no other way to survive, and that faith gave her the one thing essential to life—hope. And hope breeds expectancy. So Mother lived from day to day, waiting to see what God would do.

I cannot tell you all that my father must have felt during those days. He would express raging anger one minute and a flippant "I-don't-care" attitude the next. Sometimes he would appear strong and in control. During those times he would talk enthusiastically about continuing his work on a smaller scale without the complications of a large office, which inevitably depersonalized things and, to his way of thinking, made the rules more important than the people. Mother would take heart, thinking that perhaps this was God's way of slowing Daddy down, of taking him back to the basic essentials that would allow him to continue ministering without killing himself.

But then he would crumble before our eyes, retreating into a world of incredible pain and anguish beyond comfort or reason. He was like a mother bereft of her only child, or a king exiled from an empire of his own making. He mourned his loss with angry bellows and stormy silences, and we all watched with growing concern as his inward turmoil began to manifest itself in uncontrollable shaking and choking spells.

No one else was particularly aware of our situation or our battles. People were more than willing to accept the explanation that Daddy had resigned for health reasons. Most people placed us on a shelf labeled "inactive" and moved on. This struck home with me about a year after Daddy resigned, when I left home for my first year of college. During the first few days we were all getting acquainted, and I was inevitably introduced as Bob Pierce's daughter. "Oh," said one touchingly sincere girl, "I was so sorry to hear about your dad. When did he die?"

Daddy's disassociation with World Vision didn't happen with the slash of the pen, but rather it came gradually over a period of months. In the spring of 1968, Daddy and Mother went overseas on a "Goodbye Tour," visiting Korea, Formosa, Hong Kong, and Japan. As the time drew near to return home, Daddy began talking about making an unscheduled stop in Vietnam. Mother argued against it. Not only would she have to fly home alone, but she had a gut feeling that he shouldn't go. But Daddy was adamant; he was uncertain if he would have another opportunity.

A few days before they were to go their separate ways, the phone rang. Mother heard Sharon's distant voice.

"Hi, Mama. Is Daddy there?"

"Yes, Darling. But what is it? Is something wrong?"

"No. Yes. I love you, Mama. But can I please talk to Daddy?"

Mother handed the phone to him.

"Hello, Baby," Daddy said. "What's the matter?"

For the next several minutes, Mama watched the intensity of Daddy's face as he listened, sensing from his expression that he was battling within himself.

Finally he said, "Honey, I just can't come home right now. I feel I've got to go to Vietnam while I have the chance. I promise I'll get home as soon as I can, and your Mother will be home in a few days."

With that Mama took the phone. "Sweetheart, I'll catch a flight tomorrow, and I'm sure your dad won't be long. Are you all right?"

"Oh, I'm fine. And don't worry. It's all right. I guess I knew he wouldn't come." Sharon's voice was strangely flat and hollow. As soon as she hung up Mother made reservations to fly home.

In the hours between the phone call and her departure, Mother tried unsuccessfully to convince Daddy to come home. He was officially retired now, and for once in his life he was free to put his family's needs first. But he was caught up in a desperate struggle for his own survival. Somehow the Orient represented the best part of him, a part he felt in danger of losing, and his own need to hold on was greater than any outside influence.

As it turned out, Mother's dark premonition was justified. In a remote part of Vietnam, Daddy contracted paratyphoid. He lay in a coma for seven days before he was flown to a hospital in Hong Kong and treated. But any fear Mother was feeling for Daddy was quickly eclipsed by her concern for Sharon.

Arriving home, she found Sharon weak and depressed, her wrists bound, recovering from an unsuccessful attempt to take her own life. "I know you love me, Mama," she said, "but I just needed to feel Daddy's arms around me."

14 THE VALLEY OF THE SHADOW

Sharon asked Jesus into her heart when she was five years old, after hearing the Easter story in one of Mother's Child Evangelism classes. The following Sunday evening Daddy was speaking at a church in Los Angeles, and Mother and Sharon attended with him. At the close of the message, he asked those who wanted to make a public confession of their faith in Christ to raise their hands. Sharon lifted her hand, as did many others, but somehow it was hidden from Daddy's view. Later, as they were driving away from the church, Sharon asked, "Daddy, why didn't you point at me tonight when I raised my hand?" Then she burst into tears.

Immediately Daddy took her in his arms, and said, "Darling, I didn't see your hand, but Jesus did." He prayed with her, and while she was still in his arms she said, "Now, Daddy, I want to be baptitized." Since Daddy was leaving for China soon, a baptismal service was held the following Sunday for one small child. Papa and Daddy shared the joy of immersing her in the waters of baptism and of hearing her declare as she rose, "I love Jesus very, very much!"

Yes, Sharon loved Jesus, and her heart's commitment to him never could be questioned. Her copious notes in the well-worn pages of her Bible testify to her love and knowledge of God's Word. She knew she was a child of God, and she truly desired to serve him.

But a commitment to Jesus Christ is no guarantee of immunity to the disease and pain of this world. In fact, those who are most greatly used are often most viciously attacked. And what better way to wound the heart of a parent than through his child?

No one who knew Sharon would ever have suspected the terrible insecurity and sense of worthlessness she battled. Even Mother and Daddy didn't comprehend the seriousness of her struggle until it was too late. It is only as I read her many diaries, notebooks, letters, and poems that the true picture emerges.

The Sharon I remember was a bright, funny, spontaneous extrovert. She was a talented artist and a gifted writer. She loved music and would play the piano for hours. I loved to be with her because she could find humor in almost any situation, and we would laugh till our sides ached. As we grew older, the nine-year gap between us seemed to narrow.

When she was thirteen, my folks sent her to one of those elite Christian schools where gangly girls and boys are supposedly transformed into graceful ladies and gentlemen. At the time, "everyone" was sending their children there, and Daddy felt the social benefits would be invaluable. Mother hated to be deprived of Sharon's company, but she didn't want to keep her at home selfishly. So off Sharon went, a frightened, awkward little girl with a brand new set of braces on her teeth and freckles. That year away did accomplish some good, but Sharon's diary reveals that it was a painful and traumatic experience for her. There was no discussion about her going back for a second year.

During her early teen years, Sharon coasted comfortably as far as spiritual things were concerned. She knew more Scripture than most, she never missed church, and she ran with a healthy, clean-cut gang of kids. Mother and Dad wisely didn't push, allowing the Lord to move in His own time. And as Sharon later testified, he did.

It was another routine Sunday evening. Sharon and her friends sat in the back of the small sanctuary in the same seats they occupied every Sunday evening, whispering and doodling and passing notes back and forth the way seventeen-year-olds will when they are in church out of duty rather than desire. The choir began to sing the hymn of the morning, one Sharon had heard hundreds of times before. But this particular morning something extraordinary happened. As the music began, it struck something deep within Sharon's spirit, sending a chill down her spine and causing her to lean forward in her seat. Suddenly the words were not religious clichés, but the expression of ageless, wondrous truth. She felt as if she were seeing Jesus face to face for the first time, and the confrontation left her both broken and magnificently alive. Unable to wait until the end of the service, Sharon slipped downstairs and knelt on the cold basement floor. Tears of repentance streamed down her cheeks as she rededicated her life to her Lord.

Sharon had a marvelous mind, full of curiosity and clever ideas. And she had a compassionate heart. Her own failures and insecurities made her incredibly sensitive to other people's pain, and far less judgmental of their weaknesses. Like her father, Sharon never hesitated to get involved. She was always opening her home to those in need, taking in a young unwed mother one month and perhaps a friend down on her luck the next. She once said, "It's not what's in your hand that's important, but the reaching out, the touching, the caring." Sharon cared.

But she also inherited her mother's extremely romantic nature, and that, combined with her father's strong will, led her into an early marriage. When she was nineteen, she married her high school sweetheart— a quiet, gentle boy whom she loved but with whom she had little in common. It surprised no one that their relationship quickly deteriorated. The marriage lasted four years and produced one beautiful little girl, Lisa. Sharon was totally delighted with her fair-haired baby. She would often say to Mother, "She's beautiful, isn't she, Mama? I can't believe I made such a wonderful, beautiful child!"

But despite the great love and pride she felt for Lisa, the failure of the marriage scarred Sharon deeply. She never again saw herself as a person of great value. As far as she was concerned she was "used goods," and her self-deprecating attitude resulted in a disheartening series of unsuccessful relationships. It seemed that every time she reached out she was burned, and each bad experience destroyed a little more of her self-respect, leaving her all the more desperate for the love and approval that stubbornly eluded her. Sharon began to fight waves of overwhelming depression and hopelessness while fiercely clinging to her dreams of what might be. During this time she wrote incessantly, penning the world of thoughts she couldn't speak.

Then, when Sharon was twenty-five, Daddy took her to Vietnam as a war correspondent. She was to write human-interest stories from a woman's perspective for use in *World Vision* magazine, and she was heady with anticipation. Finally she had a chance to use her considerable talents to do something worthwhile.

Sharon thrived on the danger and excitement of this strange new world, likening her first helicopter ride in a combat zone to a roller coaster ride. "At first it is frightening, but then the thrill surpasses the fear and it is marvelous. . . . Of course, [avoiding enemy fire] is not a game, but each adventure is such a thrilling experience that I can't help looking forward to every moment."

Occasionally her sense of adventure overcame her common sense. One day, she and a friend decided to "hitchhike" via a military plane to the town of Dalat. They arrived to discover the terminal was nothing more than a large tent pitched in the middle of some rice paddies. They could find no transportation into town. The territory was definitely unfriendly, and the plane would not be able to return for them until the next day.

Fortunately, a friendly farmer came by who was willing to bury Sharon and her friend under his load of vegetables in his simple horse-drawn wagon for the short but nerve-racking journey into town. Once in Dalat, Sharon made her way to a missionary school, where she was lovingly cared for until she could be flown out safely the next day.

Evidently, the incident did little to dampen her enthusiasm, for shortly thereafter she wrote:

> In the weeks that I have been here the most wonderful and exciting things have occurred. I came with Big Daddy and while he was here, it was a storm of activity. He was only here a week and I can understand why the people in Vietnam say they are glad to see him come . . . and glad to see him go. We met with numerous government officials regarding proposed projects, flew out to the "fighting," inspected orphan sights, and enjoyed social invitations.

Daddy enjoyed having Sharon with him, and he felt her contributions significant enough to bring her back to Vietnam for a second trip. But even this time in Sharon's life was shaded by gnawing fears and feelings of inadequacy. In a letter to Mama she wrote:

> I have been constantly praying that God will do something new. . . . I don't really know what to ask for or how to pray. I just know I don't want to be useless. In just this one week I have seen and felt many things that have deeply moved me. . . . I don't know yet whether I'm a help or hindrance, but I'm trying to be a help.

Sharon returned from her second Vietnam trip full of anticipation and enthusiasm about the future. But her high hopes didn't last long. For reasons I don't understand, nothing was ever done with her articles. By January of the following year, she wrote to a friend confiding that she felt she was dying of boredom and frustration. She had had "the chance of a lifetime" to go overseas, and in her opinion she had done nothing with it. Now she was back where she started. "I feel so trapped, as if all my opportunities are quickly passing me by. I concede failure! What do you feel I should do? I'm dying. . . . Help!"

Sharon's personal papers and diaries are full of that desperate cry for help. Only God knows the damage that was done when suddenly she lost her daddy to a work that demanded all his thoughts, energy, and time. Robin and I never knew what it was to have Daddy home all the time, but Sharon was eight when he started traveling, and she suffered a very real sense of loss. Years later she wrote:

> I know Mom loves me. But some things a woman just can't give—one being the comfort of a man, yes, a father even, when he puts his arms around you and says everything will be O.K.

The feelings Sharon expressed were at times common to all of us kids, and Mother too. It was hard for us to believe that Daddy really understood our needs. Although we knew he loved us, he was gone too much to be involved with our everyday lives, and it was impossible to fill him in on several months' worth of life during two dinners and a trip to Disneyland. He was always careful to verbalize his concern and interest, but the life-and-death situations he was constantly dealing with must have made the problems of his healthy, well-fed children difficult to take seriously.

Yet none of us were adequately sensitive to the seriousness of Sharon's situation. Even Mother, whose life revolved around her children, was totally shocked when she arrived home to discover her daughter had slashed her wrists in an attempt to end a life she found too painful to endure.

During the next few months, Mother and Dad tried desperately to understand Sharon's problems and to find someone to help her. She spent several weeks in a sanitarium, where she appeared to pick up and take hold once again. But just as she began picking up the pieces of her life, her relationship with a man she deeply loved and hoped to marry ended in an extremely cruel and devastating way.

It was the final blow. Her overwhelming need for love and approval from the men in her life and her need to feel useful and significant drove Sharon deeper and deeper into the pit of despair. Her whole life had been spent like that little girl of long ago, earnestly waving her hand with a desperate desire to be acknowledged, but somehow always being overlooked in the crowd.

The only one who never hurt or disappointed her was the Savior she had accepted as a small child. Never in any of her writing did Sharon blame God for her failures or depict him as anything but a loving heavenly Father. Her deepest desire was to serve him, and she struggled with the conviction that here too, she had failed. Her last thoughts were a testimony to that fact.

> I love you Jesus. Oh, how I beg your forgiveness for each and every time I failed you or sinned. And if you find this last act a sin, please dear God, please forgive me for my final weakness. I love you, as you know.

On November 30, 1968, Sharon chose to be with Jesus. She was twenty-seven.

• • •

Of all the heartaches our family has endured, losing Sharon was the most painful. I'll never forget the look on Mama's face when she was told her baby was gone. Her eyes became glassy reflections of sheer horror, masked almost immediately by an angry, rebellious refusal to believe. "Get away from me! You're lying! No! My girl is all right! My girl is all right!"

Her cries followed me out into the quiet darkness. Collapsing on the lawn, I dug my fingers into the damp, cool soil, tearing up great clumps of earth and flinging them wildly in all directions while someone screamed in the distance. Later, as I lay listening to the silence, I realized that the someone was me.

The immediate responsibilities of Sharon's sudden death fell on me, for Mama could not possibly make all the arrangements and Daddy was away once again. Toward the end of the previous summer, he had flown to Basel, Switzerland, for an exhaustive series of tests at the famed University Hospital. They discovered that the very core of his nervous system was completely exhausted, and the process of rebuilding it would be lengthy and complicated. He wrote:

> I must remain in the hospital for shots of daily
> insulin, and have to stay under observation for
> side effects. Now that the physical impairment
> is clearly identified and under treatment, I

will begin psychiatric treatment for two hours regularly each week. Since they have found something they can physically treat, I do not object to psychiatric treatment.

Cheerful is the news that I can be better than anytime in the past ten years with completion of this treatment.

Not so cheerful is the news that all this is caused by over-exhaustion emotionally the past 21 years. The doctors expect me to keep disengaged from emotional tension for twelve months after the strong medical treatment.

The doctors' desire to keep Daddy emotionally disengaged almost kept them from telling him about Sharon's death. As it was, he was allowed to come home for only one day, the day of the funeral. That night Mother, Daddy, Robin, and I huddled together in front of the den fireplace.

"I want you to pack up and come to Switzerland," Daddy said. "I may have to stay in Basel for as long as a year for treatments as an outpatient. I'll rent a chalet and we'll all be together. Come soon. I need you!" His voice broke with tearful emotion despite the heavy medication the doctors had prescribed to insure that he would not become overly distressed. Mama nodded, and we all moved closer together as plans were discussed.

The next day we watched Daddy board the plane for Switzerland, comforted by the fact that it was only a temporary separation. Soon we'd all be together, with time to share our mutual sorrow, to encourage and strengthen one another, and with God's help to discover the new direction we were to go as a family.

But something happened between that night in December when Daddy entreated us to join him and the day we stepped off the plane in Basel the following February. While we applied for passports, got shots, packed, and arranged to close the house up for a year, Daddy continued to receive treatments with mind-controlling, personality-changing drugs aimed at counteracting the "definite setback in the vegetative [autonomic nervous] system" he had experienced due to the "past few weeks of shock and sorrow," as he put it in one of his letters.

Whatever effect the drugs had on Daddy's mind, the man who picked us up at the Basel airport was a stranger we neither knew nor understood. For him, much of the past had been blocked out medically. From the beginning he was uncomfortable with us, finding us painful intruders into the safety of the little world into which he had escaped—a world totally isolated from pain, disappointment, guilt, the responsibility of yesterday, and the frightening uncertainty of tomorrow. In this world there was only today and, as Daddy repeated several times in his letters, "I can only survive by living from day to day."

The first sign that things were out of kilter was our peculiar living arrangement. Daddy didn't rent a chalet, as he had promised. Instead, he put Mother and me in an apartment downstairs from the small bachelor one in which he was living. His cramped quarters made it appear more practical for Robin to room with him, and the floor that separated him from Mother and me became a convenient line of demarcation across which we were free to visit but not to stay.

It didn't take long for it to become painfully obvious that our coming had been a mistake. Daddy just didn't know what to do with us, and his relationship with Mother deteriorated from day to day. What had begun as a hopeful attempt to unify the family quickly became an emotional endurance test. Excerpts from Mother's journal show her pain:

> Bob's hatred of me shows up so much more here and it is hard to bear.
>
> I keep asking myself, why am I here? What chance is there of anything? When was it too late?
>
> I took a cup of coffee up to Bob's apartment. He said "Come in" and seemed cordial. I sat on the sofa and we had the only conversation thus far of significance. He discussed his belief and lack of belief—his feelings that "I expected God to take care of my children as I cared for others. He didn't," etc. . . . He seemed to leave me out of his vehemence. I listened. He then said, "I haven't talked like this for a long time." I said "It's O.K." and put my arms around him, but he was stiff.

Marilee and I joined Bob and Robin for lunch, but Bob was very depressed. He looked bad and very distant. We tried to chat and be friendly, but he would not talk. He did tell us that we would have to give up our apartment, as the landlord had called, but that we could take a few days. I know he wants us to leave, but if I go, I will say good-bye forever. I cannot work miracles.

I talked to the doctor today and he said Bob was bad, but we needed to resolve some things and he hoped we would come in together, but he didn't know if Bob would agree. I told him I would do anything I could to help the situation.

Bob and I talked at length about our being here. He is not happy we are here and feels we should leave because of expenses. He is irritated that I can feel free to stay. He says I should go home and sell the house. He just is not happy we are here. That's all.

It seems utterly impossible that the man who wept as he told us he needed us and wanted us with him and who wrote to Mother just weeks before we arrived— "We shall soon be together again. And with all my heart I pray that I may know how to be a greater joy to you"—was the same person who now was telling us to leave.

The only answer is that he was not the same man. Through the years my father had been battered and bruised, and each fresh wound required a little longer to heal. In the later years the wounds were particularly deep and painful. One would barely begin to form a scab before another would be inflicted, and then another, until emotionally he became a mass of bloody, open wounds. The final blow was Sharon. When she died, it was as if he threw his hands up in unconscious surrender, turning his back on the past and on anything and anybody even remotely connected with it.

He was unwilling to talk about Sharon, and he pronounced any display of grief on our parts morbid and unhealthy. Any mention of home or old friends was likely to inflame his temper or leave him depressed and moody. We soon found ourselves guarding each word in an attempt to avoid unpleasantness, but it was impossible. Our very presence was like salt in his wounds. Daddy's desperate attempt to deny the agony of his own soul could never succeed with us there as constant reminders of everything he was running from. For Mother, the rejection was devastating. She wrote:

> How could Bob not love me? I've never done anything to him—betrayed him, forsaken him. I bore his children, waited over twenty years for him, and when he could finally be with me, he doesn't want me. And he has nothing left.
>
> It is now the 4th of April. Sharon would be 28. Oh, Father, please, Father! Read my cries and help!

God heard those cries, and a few days later Mother and I found ourselves standing on a little patch of heaven, high on the side of a mountain near the resort town of Villars, Switzerland. Neither of us had ever heard of Francis Schaeffer or L'Abri until several friends urged us to go there. I felt a positive stirring immediately. Losing Sharon had been the first major hurt of my life and that, coupled with Daddy's peculiar behavior, had left me in desperate need of some answers. Willing to accept their urgings as more than a coincidence, but uncertain what help a total stranger might be, Mama arrived at L'Abri too cautious to be hopeful, but open to whatever God might have.

My first impression of L'Abri was an overwhelming sense of peace. As we looked out over the lush green valley to the snow-capped mountains beyond, the air itself seemed laced with a healing balm that soothed our frazzled nerves and eased the tension from our faces. The love and joy of the Lord was unmistakably apparent in the smiles that greeted us, and we knew God had brought us to someplace very special.

While I settled my things in the dormitory-style bedroom where I was to stay for the next five days, Mrs. Schaeffer led Mother upstairs to her husband's study. He was out hiking, but was due back momentarily. Mother's few minutes alone gave her a chance to acquaint herself with the man by studying his small office. The walls were lined with books from floor to ceiling, and Mother couldn't help wondering if he had really read them all. At that time she wasn't aware that he had written most of them.

Hearing footsteps coming up the stairs, Mama put on her official "Mrs. Bob Pierce" face and prepared to greet Dr. Schaeffer. But the man who entered the room caught her off guard and immediately disarmed her. Dressed in hiking boots and knickers, his rugged features framed by a mane of fine, silvery hair, with eyes brilliantly alive and interested, he took Mother's hand in a warm, solid grasp and said, "Hello, Lorraine."

The significance of those two words is still being revealed to Mother today, for in that simple greeting was the whole crux of what God wanted Mother to understand. All her life she had lived in someone else's shadow. First she was Floyd Johnson's daughter, then Bob Pierce's wife. Now, at the very time she felt the greatest failure, when it appeared that all she had stood for was meaningless and vain, God sent someone to call her by name and say, "My dear Lorraine, do you have any idea who you are? How wonderful and special and unique you are? You have been created in the image of God, for his glory and pleasure. Don't let anyone rob you of the unique specialness of being you!"

Over the next few days Dr. Schaeffer's counsel cut through Mother's insecurity and pain, stirring embers of hope and anticipation that through the years she allowed to cool in the sad assumption that she simply wasn't "one of the gifted ones." Although they didn't change the situation with Daddy or bring Sharon back, his words restored that which the past months had destroyed—her sense of self-worth.

When we left L'Abri, neither Mother nor I were the people we were when we arrived. God met us both on that mountain, providing us each with the special love and encouragement we needed. During the days of happy fellowship with the other young people staying there, and during the quiet hours of teaching and counseling with Dr. Schaeffer, I rediscovered the reality of life in Jesus. And I learned two very important things. One, that there are some things in this life for which there are no pat answers. And two, that it's all right if we don't have all the answers, because God's love and faithfulness are great enough to bridge all the gaps; as long as we keep sight of Jesus, it's not necessary always to understand.

The time with Dr. Schaeffer had helped Mother and me stand up spiritually once again. But we couldn't afford to wander around Europe indefinitely, and since Daddy wouldn't keep us with him there was nothing left to do but go home.

15 SEPARATION

Coming home from Europe was a curiously empty experience. We all needed time to recover from the emotional beating we had taken. Robin's youth and naturally sunny disposition allowed her almost immediately to push the unpleasantness of the past months into a corner of her consciousness and get on with the joyous adventure of living. I used to watch her laughing and playing and think, "How does she do it? Doesn't she see what's happened? Doesn't she understand?" I see now that Robin's laughter and unquenchable enthusiasm was a gift from the Lord to us all. She was a consistent spark of normalcy that kept us in touch with the realities of the day.

Holding onto reality became one of my most difficult battles. During the months following our trip to Europe I found myself escaping more and more into a make-believe world where Sharon still lived, where everybody loved one another, and where I felt safe and accepted.

But I was constantly being jerked back to reality. Everywhere I looked there were reminders of Sharon, and the realization that she was gone would send me into terrible bouts of depression and uncontrollable weeping. I realize now that those hours of groaning and crying expressed far more than my grief over Sharon's death; they expressed all the hurt, confusion, and frustration that had built up inside me over the years.

As for Mama—well, she went on being Mama, holding the fabric of our lives together, trying to be strong because she knew Robin and I needed her to be. Only in the night hours, after Robin and I were asleep, would she allow herself to examine her thoughts and feelings, writing everything down just as Sharon had. She wrote:

> I am here (at the beach) with my two girls for a week. It seems I am not gaining any strength, knowing any direction, at all. The weeks and months go by. I don't beseech God. Perhaps, until I do, I'll go on day after day—dry, alone—in this "away world" where only I can be with all that has happened to smack my being within so totally.

As is often the case, distance and time began to put things back into perspective. Mother had been through much with Daddy and had seen God miraculously intervene too many times in their relationship to feel that things would not eventually work out. She knew Daddy had not been himself much of the time we had been together. And despite her emotional lows, she never doubted that when Daddy was healed physically and emotionally, their relationship would be restored as God once again led them out of a troubled time of testing to a new plateau of ministry and blessing.

Her confidence was bolstered by Daddy's renewed correspondence. On July 23, 1969, he wrote:

I am homesick for you and Robin and Marilee. The medical treatment ending, my thoughts are overwhelmingly of home and you. My nerves are steady now. Only my mind is still unclear. It is unclear to me how to go about finding a new meaning in the business of doing God's will.

John Haggai has offered me the job of being chancellor of the Arosa International Training Institute starting September 15 and meantime has asked me to go with him to India for two conferences in Delhi and Bangalore starting August 7.

I know with certainty that there is no meaning to life without Christ at its center, and I am torn between the desire to come home—with nothing in view to work at—or taking this apparently open door with John. To regain sanity it is necessary to be employed for the Lord.

Please let me receive your thoughts at this time and any ideas you have.

Shortly after that letter arrived, Mother received a call from the board of Food for the World, a small organization under the auspices of World Literature Crusade. They were looking for someone to take over the work, and they wanted to know if Daddy would be interested.

A small organization Daddy could take in any direction he felt led—the package seemed to have Daddy's name written all over it! Mother could hardly wait to contact him. His immediate response was subdued, but Mother encouraged him to see the possibilities. At least it was a start.

In early fall of 1969, Daddy moved home. On his way, he stopped in Los Angeles to sign papers making him president of an organization with a net worth of about eighteen dollars. Eventually he would change the name to "Samaritan's Purse" and broaden the concept of the ministry from supplying food to aiding all types of needs on an individual or small scale.

For my father, coming home meant far more than searching out a new life; it meant facing up to the old one. While Mother, Robin, and I had gone through the stages of mourning Sharon's loss together, gradually finding the constant reminders of her more sweet than bitter, Daddy had avoided such confrontations almost entirely. And while the three of us had grown accustomed to our disassociation from World Vision, Daddy hadn't even begun to tackle that emotional and psychological mountain. For over a year he had been carefully sheltered and protected, relieved of the responsibility of thinking or feeling. If something hurt him, he was given emotional painkillers. If something upset him, the doctors prescribed it away. Now he came back to a house in which Sharon's voice still seemed to echo and to a city where all roads seemed to lead to World Vision. The atmosphere at home was charged with tension. Mother was overly solicitous, like an insecure child trying too hard to please. And Daddy was immaculately polite, his stiffly proper responses putting up a wall more impenetrable than his anger ever had.

None of us knew how to break through that wall. I suppose we all felt that in time Daddy would just snap out of it and gradually things would get back to normal. But "normal" didn't really exist for Daddy any more, and that realization must have filled him with fear and desperation.

One day he announced he was going to paint the house—all by himself. He bought brushes, ladders, buckets, and gallons of paint, attacking the project as if his life depended on it. For two weeks he sanded and scraped and painted, working up to fourteen hours a day, setting up big spotlights so he could paint after dark. Having no understanding of the need that birthed his obsession, we all laughed at his extraordinary behavior. My heart still breaks as I envision the man, spotlighted high on a ladder, a painter's cap pulled over his graying curls, his face and arms spattered with paint, dripping with perspiration despite the chilly night air, feverishly painting a call for help no one had ears to hear.

I enrolled in a drama workshop in Hollywood, determined to become the first Christian Sarah Bernhardt.

Mother and Daddy did not feel good about the direction I was going, and I knew it. But in my own way I had begun to rebel. I didn't smoke, drink, or swear. I was a virgin and would remain one until I married. And I truly desired to serve the Lord—but my way, not His. And therein lay the seeds of my destruction, the weak link that left me vulnerable to deception.

The first day of drama class I met a young man who was ten years older than I, who had been married before, and who didn't know how to say "good morning" without using a four-letter word. But he was also tall, dark, handsome, remarkably talented, and utterly charming. He both frightened and fascinated me, and before I knew it I had invited him home for dinner.

Mother and Daddy immediately saw what attracted me to Scott. He was funny and bright and had a vulnerable quality that made Mother want to "mother" him. He began coming to the house often, and we would have long discussions about the Bible and Jesus. He seemed sincerely interested and open, so my folks let him keep coming. But they also kept an anxious eye on our relationship, continually cautioning me not to get too involved.

My response was always the same. "Don't worry; Scott's only a friend. I want him to meet Jesus. I'm not going to fall in love. I can handle it."

And so, as I struggled to stay emotionally unattached, Mother and Dad sought to somehow reconnect the lines of communication that years of separation and heartbreak had severed.

It was February 1970, one of those bright, clear winter days when the air is clean, the sky is blue, and the mountains appear so close you could touch them. Robin was out playing with a friend and I was reading when I heard loud voices. It seemed Daddy had taken all of Mother's credit cards out of her wallet without her knowledge, and Mother wanted them back. The argument was hot and heavy, with Daddy roaring that Mother spent too much money and Mother strongly denying the accusations, pointing out that he had no idea what it cost to feed and clothe two growing girls.

This certainly wasn't a new tune around our house. But this particular day things got out of hand. The credit cards were the spark that lit the fuse on a whole keg of dynamite, and as the smoke cleared, Mother and I watched Daddy walk out the door, suitcase in hand.

The next few weeks were a collage of emotional crises—one overlapping another in a crazy patchwork of hurt and anger and fear. We all expected Daddy to move home at any moment. Then one day we were informed that all our credit had been cut off, including the market and the drug store, and the next day the phone company called to say they'd been instructed to disconnect our telephone. Gradually it began to sink in that Daddy was serious; he had made the break.

And yet he didn't disappear from our lives. He moved into a motel only five minutes away and called or came over whenever he felt like it. Two weeks after he left, he sent Mother a beautiful valentine, signing it with love. In April he wrote several letters from overseas, addressing them to "My Beloved Family" and making statements like, "I am thinking of you constantly, praying for you and loving you, each one, with all my heart."

It was his inconsistency, his constant contradictions that wore Mother down emotionally and physically. For weeks she carried that valentine around with her. It was evidence that Daddy still loved her and that their relationship was salvageable, but it was a flimsy defense against Daddy's adamant insistence that she see a lawyer.

Day after day, Robin and I watched Mother agonize over the situation. She was unable to conceal the total devastation of her soul. At times it would be so bad that Robin would run to me for reassurance that Mama was going to be all right, her little face pinched with worry and her eyes filled with pain and questions I couldn't answer. At times like that I wanted to grab Daddy and scream, "Why are you doing this? We love you! We need you! You're killing her. Stop it! Stop. Just stop!"

But of course, I never did. During this time Scott became an increasingly important person in my life. He was always there to encourage me and hold me, his presence providing strength and security. While concerned friends and loved ones did their best to make me see the danger, I continued to deny that there was anything serious between us—right up until the day in July 1970, when Scott and I eloped.

Two months later Daddy took Mother to court, and they were legally separated.

• • •

Mother never recovered from the fact that Daddy took her to court. She accepted Sharon's death because she had no choice. She accepted my marriage because she didn't want to lose me. But the legal separation was something Mama never accepted.

Some people said they had seen it coming for years. Certainly the relationship had had its ups and downs from the very beginning, and the pressures of the last ten years had been particularly damaging.

Back in May of 1966, Mama had written Daddy a letter she never intended to send. It read, in part:

> I've just finished reading some of the letters you wrote to me, dated from 1947 to 1958. What ever happened to those people, you and me, who wrote such letters? How could those years (lovely, trying, testing, tiring, yet victorious) be ignored, tossed aside as if they counted for so little, when in truth they were the most valuable, perhaps, we will have ever lived? Anyway, I was glad to be reminded of the past, realizing the tremendous investment of lives and faith and love. It's too bad we lost out somewhere, and the words on paper, from us both, couldn't have

continued. What a wonderful inheritance for our children. What a story they tell.

At times, Daddy seemed to be reaching out. On their thirtieth wedding anniversary, he presented Mother with a beautiful pearl ring, writing, "You are a pearl of great price. I wanted to give you at least one good pearl with the luster and glow I pray we may have in the rest of life together."

Recognizing that much of their problem was a lack of communication, not a lack of love, Mother sought counseling during the mid-sixties. It was hard for her to admit they needed this kind of help, and even harder to break free of the thought that truly spiritual people sought help only from God, not men. But she was determined to find some answers for their problems. Unfortunately, the verdict was always the same: "We can do no more until your husband comes in with you." This Daddy would never do.

Now the long hard years of holding on seemed to mean nothing. Over thirty years of marriage had been dismissed with the bang of a gavel. Alimony, child support, Robin cut up and passed out evenly (you get her Christmas, I get her Thanksgiving). It was a nightmare from which, for the next eight years, Mother would stubbornly insist she would one day wake up.

For Daddy, on the other hand, the separation seemed to take an enormous burden off his shoulders. Now he had only to provide those things prescribed by law, and he was free to pop in and out of our lives as he saw fit.

For the next few years that's what he did, calling at the last moment one or two nights a week when he was home to invite us to dinner, knowing that even if we had dinner on the stove we'd turn it off and rush to be with him. I very seldom turned down an opportunity to be with my dad, even though occasionally I resented his last-minute appearance.

Daddy always joined us on holidays or special occasions, even moving home for the week between Christmas and New Year's for the first few years. You would have thought we were expecting royalty the way Mama would fuss—rearranging the furniture in his room, stocking the cupboards with his favorite foods, doing everything she could think of to make the house comfortable and appealing, and constantly beseeching God for the one gift her heart desired—her husband home again. Every Christmas her heart would swell with hope as she watched him pull into the drive and take his suitcase out of the car. And every New Year's Day that heart would break as she watched him walk out the door once again.

As the months passed and Daddy showed no sign of changing his mind, Mother vacillated between feelings of hopeless despair and indignant anger. In March of 1971, she wrote:

Difficult, painful days are these. I was able to unload my heavy heart a bit but there's so much that pains and hurts that where a place is made empty by talk and tears, it just fills up with more of the same. It is like all the tears and crying washed nothing at all away. . . .

[I have always believed that] God is our partner and at work, and that things will work out in God's way, that no matter how things appear to be, nothing can keep my marriage from healing. Now, I'm asked, "Why?" Why should I expect this miracle any more than the times when God just doesn't intervene in situations?

All I know is I couldn't, just couldn't let go.

Close friends and family, including Robin and me, began urging Mother to give up for the sake of her own sanity and health. Although our advice was motivated by loving concern, it reeked of faithlessness to Mother, and as tempting as it was to walk away from the whole mess, she could never bring herself to turn her back on God's Word. She continued to stand on his promises, even though as time passed it became an increasingly lonely place to stand.

It seems that I am standing alone in my resistance against this breakup of my marriage. The few I have sought counsel from have not pointed to the Word, just to our human circumstances. Where are God's people who will stand with me in resistance against this evil?

In the meantime, Daddy determined to get on with his life, like a person trying to put a puzzle together with half the pieces missing. He started working again, producing a film for Lillian Dickson and taking the first steps to get Samaritan's Purse off the ground. His name still carried weight, and the world was full of people who loved him and considered it an honor to help him.

He found great release in travel and accepted many invitations to go overseas. But he never moved his home base to the Orient, as he often had said he was going to do. Instead, he kept an apartment close to home. And while he was away he wrote beautiful letters, as if the physical distance freed him to draw near to us without fear.

Although most of the time I was not there to see his tears or hear his cries, I know that no one suffered more than my father during those years. Doctors can make their physical diagnoses. Psychiatrists can make their psychological observations. Theologians can expound on spiritual implications. But only God sees the whole picture. Only He knows why Daddy was driven to cut himself off from the ones who loved and needed him the most, and whom he so desperately needed in return.

I sat many times with my father trying to make some sense out of things, and I heard him say over and over, "I love your mother. I've always loved her. She's the only woman I ever have loved or ever will love. But I just can't come back." He'd look so lost and alone, nothing like the strong, assured, man-of-the-world image he presented most of the time, and I would ache for him.

At other times, the mere mention of Mother's name would send him into venomous rages that would soon spread to World Vision, Sharon, and any others who had hurt him. He had made Mother a symbol of all the failures and disappointments he could not face up to. Leaving her was his way of exorcising the ghosts of the past.

16 BLESSINGS AND HEARTACHES

So far I have written only the human facts, not the spiritual reality of our situation. For when you know God and are living within the realm of his power, authority, and abundant mercy, reality has little to do with circumstances.

Reality during those years was God's unfailing provision, his tender watchfulness, his continuous displays of faithfulness and concern, and his constant reassurance that although he had not seen fit to spare us this walk through the valley, he would stay close beside us every step of the way. Ultimately, the victory would be ours.

Reality was God's unwavering compassion for his servant, a man he had called to the front lines of the heaviest warfare and who now bore the scars. Understanding as none of us could the toll the many battles had taken, God never removed his blessing from my father's ministry. On the day he died, Daddy's bags were packed and ready to go as God continued to use him to touch others in his name.

Reality was God's healing even as he allowed Satan to continue to plague Daddy's body and mind. In 1972 the muscles in one of Daddy's eyes stopped functioning. The doctor said this was caused by the high blood sugar Daddy had many years before, and the muscle failure was usually irreversible in one his age. For months he wore a patch to cover the useless eye.

One day Daddy came to the house, as he often did. Looking at him, I just knew God wanted to heal his eye. I asked him if I could pray for him and he agreed. I laid hands on him as I had seen others do and prayed a simple but sincere prayer, honestly believing that when I was finished Daddy would remove his patch to find the eye restored. When I finished the eye was unchanged, but Daddy took me in his arms and through tears he said, "None of my children has ever prayed for me like that. It means so much to me. I love you, Sweetheart, and I thank you with all my heart."

Two weeks later, Daddy was sitting at his desk working on correspondence when his secretary walked in and stopped suddenly. "Your eye! Dr. Bob, your eye!"

Unconsciously, Daddy had pushed his patch up to make reading easier, too deep in thought to notice that both eyes were functioning normally. Miraculous healing in the midst of infirmity was the reality of our situation.

Reality was God's hand on Robin and me, holding us steady and directing us through years that would influence the rest of our lives. Robin was twelve when Daddy left—a dangerous time for a child to be suddenly left without a father's influence. Yet Robin never used her family situation as an excuse to rebel or to reject the principles by which she was reared. Instead, it was frequently her childlike expressions of faith that would stoke the dwindling flame of belief within Mother's heart at a particularly dark hour. As she watched Robin grow from a youngster to a beautiful, godly young woman, Mother never ceased to be conscious of the special gift God had given her in this child of her autumn years.

Reality was God's unfailing encouragement of, and provision for, Mother throughout those long, lonely years. Dr. Schaeffer's admonition to allow God to show her who she was and to step out as a person with something to offer spurred Mother into action. Coming home from Europe, she volunteered to work with the young people in her church, starting with junior high and then high school.

To her amazement, the young people responded to her in an unusually open manner, sensing that she really cared. She discovered she had a special gift of communicating the truth of God's Word in a way they could accept and relate to. Many began coming to her with their questions and problems, calling her "Mom" and bringing their unsaved friends to meet her. A number of young men and women came to know Jesus as a result of Mother's love and interest.

As Mother gained confidence in her own abilities, God broadened her ministry. In 1972 and 1973 she organized and oversaw a large portion of the Southern California Women's Great Commission Prayer Crusade, a vision God gave Vonette Bright to organize women to pray for their country. That movement eventually gave birth to our National Day of Prayer.

Soon after Daddy left, Mother decided to attend an art class with a friend. She had always enjoyed sketching but had never considered her talent important enough to develop. Now, at fifty, she didn't care if people laughed or found her efforts unworthy. She needed something to keep her mind off her problems. To her surprise, she found that when she sat down in front of a canvas she forgot all else. She could sit for hours, lost in the patient blending of color and form. And she was good. A sense of accomplishment was an unexpected bonus as friends began requesting paintings by "Lorraine."

Yes, the reality of our lives had little to do with the sticky web of confusion and pain in which the enemy had caught us. And through it all the most unbelievable miracle of all was the gift of faith God gave Mother—her belief that the whole structure of lies, misunderstandings, bitterness and unforgiveness would one day collapse as totally as a house of cards. Year after year, her confession never changed: "I don't understand why God has allowed this to happen, but I know as surely as I live that he will not let it end this way. The longer we go and the more hopeless the situation, the greater the victory will be. And when that day comes, we'll climb to the highest mountaintop together and shout, 'God has healed our family!'"

But while God's Word and his Spirit kept reassuring us that even though the battle was bloody, the war was already won, Satan continued to wreak havoc with our relationship with Daddy, breaking down communications and twisting the simplest events into devastating experiences. Mother, Robin, and I frequently found ourselves being rebuked for things we had never said or done, or being chided for not doing something we had done. Even simple conversation became difficult; our words were twisted between the speaker's mouth and the listener's ears. Over and over again our best attempts to communicate ended in anger and tears.

It was obvious that none of us could stand the strain much longer. I suggested that Mother, Robin, and I write Daddy a letter, and since it was my idea it was left to me to do the honors.

September 20, 1973

Dear Daddy,

    After much talk and prayer over the present family situation, Robin, Mother, and I have decided the wisest thing to do is to write this letter. . . .

    The first important thing which needs to be stated is that we all love you, and our need of your love and participation in our lives as husband and father has never been greater. We pray constantly for the day the Lord, in His great mercy and wisdom, will miraculously unite us in His perfect bond of love, and make us what we need to be to one another, to make us a family in the most beautiful sense of the word.

But as the time goes by and the distance between us grows greater, we are filled with an overpowering feeling of despair and frustration, as our best intentions are turned time and again into something hurting and ugly. . . .

Obviously, we cannot go on this way. You and Mother are slowly dying before Robin's and my eyes. Robin is frightened and confused, and filled with feelings she can't cope with. And I, at this particular time of great need and searching, find the whole situation unbearable. (Scott had left me a few months before and our marriage would soon end.)

We all believe in and look forward to the day that the Lord will heal the wounds and wash away all the bitterness, resentment, and pain, and help us to so totally forgive and love each other that the old things will become new! He can and will do this for us, Daddy, but only as we allow Him to. We three are most willing to kneel right now and submit all the "old" things to the Lord. All we need to start this new life is you and your honest desire to do the same. But until the time when you feel this is what you want, too, let's not hurt each other any more by pretending things are right when they aren't. It hurts too much to have you pop into our lives for a dinner or a holiday and then pop out again. We know you feel the confusion and pain of not having your rightful place and authority in our lives when we are together. But surely you can understand that a man must take his place and accept his authority on a fulltime basis, as husband and father, in the way the Lord ordained.

The result of my well-intentioned meddling was a year of silence. That had not been the result we'd hoped for, but I am not at all sure it wasn't the result God wanted. We all had received an emotional thrashing over the past years, and Mother and Daddy were showing signs of physical weakening from the constant friction. It was almost as if God gave us a year of "R and R," removing us from the combat zone so that even though the war still raged around us, we were out of the direct line of fire.

Robin was the first to break the silence, writing a letter to say how much she loved and missed him.

Daddy responded immediately, calling Robin to say he loved her more than his own life, and that he would take her to lunch so they could have time to talk. He also said he felt things would be better for us all. Two days later he called to say he was leaving the country, and the lunch never happened. But the ice had been broken, and during the next few months we took the first shaky steps toward reestablishing relations.

I found out that Daddy was speaking at a church in North Hollywood, close to my apartment in Van Nuys, and I called and asked him if I could come and bring someone special I wanted him to meet. The previous July I had met a Bible college student named Robert John Dunker. The second time I saw him the Lord told me we would marry (though it took Bob considerably longer to get the message!). And so on a Sunday evening in early November, the two Bobs in my life met for the first time. I hadn't seen Daddy in over a year.

The following May, Daddy walked me down the aisle and sat next to Mother as Bob and I became one in Jesus. It was the last time they would be together for over three years.

17 LEUKEMIA!

Bob and I returned from our honeymoon to find Daddy admitted to Scripps Clinic for tests. We drove to La Jolla, planning to rescue him from the hospital for a couple of hours to have a nice dinner and tell him about our idyllic sojourn from Carmel to San Francisco to Tahoe. But while he had sounded gung-ho on the telephone, Daddy barely had enough strength to glance through our wedding pictures, and when he tried to get out of bed the color drained from his face and his legs wouldn't hold him. His doctor stepped in to say they should have some definite results in a day or two, and Daddy promised to call as soon as he heard.

When the call came, the tone of his voice seemed to indicate good news. "Well, Baby, Daddy's got leukemia. Looks like I'll be going home soon!"

Leukemia! The very word sent a chill down my spine. And yet Daddy said it so casually that I began to wonder if I was overreacting. I remember feeling like he wanted me to congratulate him rather than commiserate with him.

It was my father's total lack of self-pity or fear of dying that allowed those around him to accept his impending death without discomfort or self-consciousness. To be absent from the body was to be present with the Lord—perfected, whole, and healthy. But he was too vital to simply lie down and die. In fact, the news of his illness seemed to recharge him, filling him with the determination to pack every second of life God gave him with ministry. He continued to travel extensively, coming home for several weeks of radiation or chemotherapy; then taking off again for some primitive part of the world. At no time did Daddy permit his illness to dictate the boundaries of his world. January 1976 found him in besieged Saigon, helping friends get out of the country. During that time he sent Mother this telegram:

Mrs. Bob Pierce,

I love you. Aware your prayers as we spent dangerous week in North. Huge refugee program developing. Keep praying.

Love, Bob.

Perhaps his words of love sparked a new flicker of hope in Mother's heart. Certainly nothing else offered any encouragement. They hadn't seen one another since the week of my wedding.

The complete severing of all contact with Daddy except through legal channels was very difficult for Mother. She desperately needed someone in whom she could confide, and she had no one she felt she could be totally honest with. So she began seeing a Christian psychologist, a compassionate, intelligent woman who quickly became more friend than doctor.

One day they were talking and Mother expressed again how much she wanted Daddy to move home. "He shouldn't be alone through these days. He should be surrounded by his family and loved ones. He doesn't have to take me back as a wife. He doesn't even have to talk to me if he doesn't want to. I'll move into the back bedroom and he can have our room. If only he'd let me take care of him, nurse him, be close to him. That's all I want. I'd settle for that."

To Mother's total shock, the psychologist picked up her phone and said, "Send Dr. Pierce in, please."

Mother watched with open mouth as Daddy entered the room and seated himself tensely across the room. Fortunately, the doctor did most of the talking, repeating Mother's invitation almost word for word. When she was through, Daddy firmly declined, saying that under no circumstances would he consider such an arrangement. As if in a bad dream, Mother watched him walk out the door, unable to believe what had just happened.

It's hard to explain what happened to Robin and me during Daddy's last three years. It is human nature to adapt to even the most unnatural and painful circumstances, and after a while we simply began accepting what we were helpless to change. We had become strangers to Daddy, the sands of time having gradually buried our common ground as we were remolded and shaped by daily events that didn't touch often enough to interweave.

Perhaps if we had had a better father-daughter foundation to begin with, we wouldn't have lost touch. But there never had been time for cultivating the kind of soul-level relationship some fathers have with their children. My image of my father had always been more heavily influenced by who he was and what he did than by his personal involvement in my life, simply because he wasn't there most of the time. And, as Sharon expressed, when he was there we felt inhibited about sharing our inner feelings and needs, fearing he would find them shallow or, worse yet, a burden. So even in the best of times there were parts of each of us that Daddy never saw. And of course, there was much about him that we never understood.

As time passed it became increasingly hard for Robin and me to figure out where we fit in Daddy's life. His illness had made him dependent upon a few close associates who seemed to form a kind of adoptive family in which we had no part. In the first few months of his illness, Bob and I offered to be of service in any way we could, but we were always told, "Oh, don't bother. So-and-so will do it." Finally we got out of the habit of offering, an unfortunate mistake that Daddy interpreted as rejection and lack of concern on our parts.

A chief cause of our confusion and worry was Daddy's order that his doctor release no information to any member of the family. The doctor strictly obeyed, refusing to answer either written or telephoned inquiries about Daddy's condition. Since we could get no official word as to how he was doing, we were vulnerable to any rumor or bit of misinformation to drift down the grapevine.

On one particularly traumatic day in the fall of 1976, Mother received a call from an old friend saying he'd just heard that Daddy had passed away while overseas, and he wanted to express his sympathies. Well, Daddy was away, and none of us had heard from him or about him for weeks, so there was a possibility that the story was true. Calls were placed all over the Orient until Daddy was located, very much alive. Needless to say, the incident left Mother shaken, and Robin and I determined to protect her from any future unnecessary anguish.

Daddy himself was our main source of information. Although my relationship with him was about as stable as a vial of nitroglycerin, I was determined to keep the door open, and I would call or write every few weeks to see how he was. At times the news would be good. The treatments seemed to be working and he would feel relatively strong and well. But frequently the report was totally negative. His blood count was up, the treatments were having little effect, and the doctors gave him only weeks to live.

At first such news would send us all into an emotional tailspin, Robin and I jumping each time the phone rang, Mother grappling with the realization that Daddy might die, leaving her to live with the pain and failure of the past eight years. But as the months passed, it became apparent to all of us that something extraordinary was happening.

The doctor's original prognosis had been six months to a year. But Daddy passed the one-year mark and then the two and three-year anniversary of the discovery of his illness, surviving several crises that should have killed him. The doctors began to take note. One young specialist told Daddy shortly before he died, "You may not be aware of it, Dr. Pierce, but every doctor on the floor is keeping daily tabs on your progress. Around here you're considered something of a miracle."

Daddy believed God continued to sustain him because he had more work for him to do. And indeed he did. He continued to bless Daddy's ministry all over the world through his work with Samaritan's Purse.

But the Spirit of God ministered something quite different to our hearts. We believed that God would not release Daddy to go home until somehow, some way, the family situation had been redeemed.

While God's heart is broken over the millions of lost, starving, homeless people in the world, he is no less moved by the desperate cries of a torn and bleeding family. To have taken Daddy home without first healing the gaping wounds inflicted upon this family would have been totally contrary to God's nature and character.

Although our hearts had received the promise, it became increasingly difficult for our heads to comprehend exactly how this restoration would take place. Daddy absolutely refused to even speak to Mother, much less see her. "I never expect to see your Mother on this earth again," he would say. "We'll just wait until we get to heaven. We'll have our glorified bodies, there will be no more pain, and we'll be able to love and accept one another in perfect love."

In December of 1977, Robin married Victor Ruesga, a Christian boy who was studying to be a landscape contractor. Daddy was seriously ill and was hospitalized at the time of the wedding, so he missed the opportunity to walk his youngest down the aisle.

Eager to make it up to Robin, he stopped by the newlyweds' apartment on New Year's Day, intending to discuss an appropriate wedding gift. Somehow Mother's name came up, eliciting from Daddy an unexpected and uncalled for recounting of all her weak points. Robin responded by asking Daddy to please not talk about Mother like that in her home. Taking her request as a rebuke, he stormed out of the apartment.

Later that day I called Daddy to wish him a happy New Year. Unaware that he was still seething from the earlier confrontation, I spent thirty minutes trying everything in my power to avoid an argument. However, it became clear that I was fighting a losing battle, and I hung up—totally perplexed as to how my New Year's greeting had ended in such disaster.

So 1978 arrived to find Daddy pretty much alienated from all three of us. Mother and Robin were at a loss as to how to approach him, but I had an advantage they didn't have—his granddaughter. Michelle Lorraine Dunker arrived on November 5, 1976. A few weeks before, Daddy and I had argued, and as a result, Michelle was nearly eight months old before he came to see her.

I'll never forget watching him get out of his car and walk up our front drive. His steps were slow and unsteady, like those of a very old man. I hadn't seen him for months, and I was unprepared for the change. He looked so fragile, his face unnaturally flushed from the chemotherapy he'd been receiving.

I had prayed all morning that Michelle would respond well. Babies are very unpredictable at eight months of age, and Daddy was a total stranger to her. But an angel must have whispered in her ear, for at her first sight of him she broke into a big, gurgling grin, flashing all eight "toofers" and raising a pair of chubby, dimpled arms in his direction. His eyes filled with tears, as did mine, and he announced with grandfatherly pride, "I have a picture of this baby taken sixty-two years ago. She looks just like me!"

I probably wouldn't have had the courage to keep knocking on the door of Daddy's life if I hadn't had Michelle. But she was the one person in our family who represented pure joy and love with no painful associations, and I was determined that he was going to have at least this grandchild in the loneliness of what might be his last year.

18 THE MIRACLE

In July and August of 1978, Bob and I had the opportunity to be with Daddy on several occasions. The leukemia, the radiation, the chemotherapy, and the experimental nuclear treatments he received had taken their toll. His complexion varied from sunburned pink to chalky gray, most of his hair had fallen out, and although his face and stomach were bloated, his arms and legs were pathetically thin. And yet every time we saw him he was nattily dressed, his shoes were shined, and a silver-gray hairpiece made up for what he had lost. All things considered, he was still a fine-looking man.

During one visit in late August, Daddy talked openly about his life and death, saying how sorry he was for any pain he had caused Robin and me, and that he loved us and wished things had been different. "I only wish you both had had a chance to really know your Daddy," he said in a broken, husky voice.

When we parted that night I knew there was little time left. I thought about calling Mother, but I knew if I told her he was really fading she would try to contact him, and I feared it would lead to one more nasty, painful confrontation. I didn't want it to end that way, for both of their sakes, so I didn't say anything to her.

But Daddy obviously wanted to see Robin, so I called to tell her the situation, encouraging her to contact him immediately. No sooner had we hung up than Robin called Mother to tell her about Daddy. That phone call set off a chain of events that some will call coincidence or luck. But as far as we're concerned, it was pure miracle.

Mother's first inclination was to call Daddy's doctor even though, in the past, the doctor had never agreed to talk with her. This time, though, Daddy's regular doctor was on vacation. A young doctor was in charge, and as he was unaware of the family conflicts, he was more than happy to talk to Dr. Pierce's wife. From him Mother learned that Daddy's most recent treatments had been totally ineffectual, and his life expectancy was less than two weeks.

The news shot through Mother's being like an electric current. Daddy was dying. Picking up the phone, she attempted to reach him. Learning he was out of town, she had to content herself with leaving a message for him to call her back.

The top of the page in Mother's Daily Light for September 1, 1978, reads, "Bob called me today!" The fact that Daddy responded to her call is the second major link in our chain of miraculous events. They talked for an hour and a half, and although the first half of their conversation came uncomfortably close to being the disaster I had feared, the fact that they talked so long is significant in itself.

For years, at the least sign of conflict or disagreement Daddy had tuned out. We all understood his need to avoid any extreme emotional stress, but it did leave us—particularly Mother—in a frustrating and helpless position as we saw the years confuse and exaggerate so many problems that open, honest interaction could have resolved.

Mother and Dad's phone conversation could easily have dissolved into one more unsatisfying "non-communication" where both talk and neither listens. But God had decided that this was the moment to blow away some of the fog and begin clarifying issues that for years had been wrapped in layers of self-pity, unforgiveness, disappointment, and confusion. Oh, voices rose and angry feelings were expressed, but instead of throwing out accusations and complaints like hand grenades and then running for cover, my parents stood their ground, facing one another with an openness they hadn't experienced for many years.

Daddy's overpowering volume and verbal dexterity no longer intimidated Mother. The knowledge that she might never have another opportunity to speak her heart gave her a courage and an authority she had been incapable of in the past. And Daddy responded with equal honesty, taking time to really listen and think about what she was saying.

Of course, that conversation didn't resolve the problems thirty-five years had created. But it did open a door that had been slammed shut and bolted tight.

And it gave Mother the opportunity to say, "I love you. The girls love you. We are your family and always will be. We represent you and belong to you, and nothing will ever change that."

At the end of the conversation Daddy asked, "What is it you want, Lorraine?"

Mama answered, "Before you go home, I want you to call your children and grandchildren and me to come be with you and let the family be together one last time. Don't give me an answer now. I want you to have time to think and pray about it. Call me when you have an answer."

A few hours later Daddy called back. "Mama, will you and the girls have dinner with me tomorrow night at six? Sheraton Universal."

Before six the next evening we pulled into the parking lot. This was one appointment for which none of us wanted to be late. We were all excited and a little nervous, but while our stomachs fluttered with butterflies, our spirits rested in calm assurance. We had enlisted the prayer support of many friends. Bob and I had asked the entire elder body at The Church On The Way to get on their knees on our behalf, and we were wonderfully conscious of God's covering and presence. Walking into the hotel lobby, we felt like we were being escorted by a guard of heavenly beings. Stopping for a moment, we formed a circle and agreed together in prayer. Then we hurried up to the suite Daddy had reserved for us.

We heard him before we saw him. Walking down the corridor toward the open door of the suite, we could hear his strained voice complaining to the management over the phone that things were not as he had requested. He had gone to the trouble of sending one of his secretaries earlier that day to insure that everything would be right, but the room had not been set up correctly. As we entered we could see his hand shake as he set the receiver back in place, and we wondered if this was a preview of things to come. But as soon as he saw us the tension eased from his face, and he gestured to us with a smile. "Come in, come in!"

Walking into that room was like coming into the warmth out of a cold, stormy night. It was as if a blanket of peace had settled over the entire evening. We could sense it immediately as each of us went to embrace Daddy. His eyes were bright with love and excitement, his pain and discomfort temporarily forgotten. Mother stood hesitantly by the door, drinking in the display of affection but too uncertain to automatically include herself in the happy reunion.

"Mama, if I could get out of this chair I'd come over there and kiss you," Daddy said, sensing her hesitation.

That was all she needed. Mama stepped across the room, bridging nine years of separation and pain, and we all watched with aching throats and tear-glazed eyes as Mother and Daddy embraced.

After that the evening flew by, each precious moment leaving an indelible impression on our hearts and minds. We talked and laughed, without the tension or uneasiness we had come to associate with our times with Daddy. It was like the past ten years hadn't happened at all. There were no apologies or attempted explanations; they weren't necessary. We loved one another. We loved being together. We were a family.

Our dining room overlooked the hills of the San Fernando Valley, and we sat at a large round table feasting on shrimp cocktail, prime rib, and good conversation. Daddy sat next to Mother, pouring her coffee and fixing it the way she liked it—with much cream and little sugar. They looked so natural together, talking, laughing, enjoying their children and taking special delight in the antics of little Michelle, who at twenty-two months had no idea of the significance of this momentous occasion.

Robin and I were both pregnant, and as we sat around the table discussing whose baby was going to be named what, Daddy commented a bit wistfully, "My, we certainly are going to have a brood, aren't we?" We knew he was thinking that he wouldn't be there to see those new grandbabies, and as the sun slipped behind the mountains, the dying light took on a sad significance.

After dinner we got out the trusty old instamatic, wanting to capture in pictures as much of the evening's joy as possible. Daddy was a good sport, smiling gamely as we grouped and regrouped around him. But the energy and effort the evening had demanded of him began to show. The effects of his medication began to wear off, and Mama was the first to recognize that for Daddy's sake our visit must come to an end.

"Bob, we know you're getting tired, and we don't want to keep you any longer than you should stay. I just want to tell you how much this evening means to the children and me. We'll remember and cherish it as long as we live, and we thank you with all our hearts." Then, after a slight hesitation she added, "Would you mind if we prayed together?"

"Not at all, Mama."

So Mother began to pray, praising God for the miracle of that night, for his faithfulness through all the years, and particularly asking his blessing and loving mercy on Daddy. As her prayer came to an end, Daddy picked it up, thanking the Lord for a lifetime of usefulness in his service and then praying for each of us by name. At one point he laid his hands on Robin's and my stomachs, weaving into the design of those yet unborn that scarlet thread of faith and service through his powerful prayers of blessing and commitment. It was a precious, holy time, and while Michelle toddled from one knee to the next, offering words of comfort and handfuls of Kleenex, we all wept openly, united in the sweet healing of tears and praise.

Daddy's prayer ended. A hush fell over the room as we all sat quietly, unwilling to disturb the sweetness of that special moment. Then Mother began singing softly, "Jesus, we just want to thank you, thank you for being so good," and we all joined in, raising our hands and voices to heaven. As that song ended, Daddy's thin but still mellow tones rang out with "Alleluia," and once again the room was filled with perfect harmony.

And so ended our evening, September 2, 1978—a night of miracles.

19 AN AFFAIR OF STATE

Lying in bed that night, I couldn't sleep. I was filled with the wonder and incredible joy of what God had done. It is easy, when you've prayed and waited for a miracle for a long time, to be caught totally off guard when God answers. It wasn't that I had stopped believing God *could* do something, but somewhere along the line I had stopped expecting that he *would* do something. Now that he had, I was awed and excited and overwhelmed with a fresh awareness of God's power.

I felt very close to Daddy. I wanted to keep touching him somehow, to continue the intimacy of the evening. So at two in the morning I slipped out of bed and wrote him a letter to thank him and to tell him how much I loved him. I mailed it the next day, a Saturday, and since the following Monday was a holiday the letter wasn't delivered until Tuesday. I'll always be sorry I didn't telephone my "thank you," for Daddy never received my note.

Early Wednesday afternoon, September 6, 1978, with all unfinished business taken care of, Jesus took my dad home. The following Monday, a memorial service was held in the great Hall of the Crucifixion-Resurrection at Forest Lawn Cemetery in Glendale, California. Nearly a thousand people came from all over the world to attend what one person described as "an affair of state in the kingdom of God." It was there that God gave me words to relate the final and perhaps the greatest miracle of my father's life.

"I'm going to talk to you out of my heart," I told the assembled crowd. "I'm going to talk to you as family because I know you all loved my daddy, and that makes you family.

"Separation and distance were not foreign to the Pierce family. All my life I experienced going to the airport and watching my father get on a plane and fly thousands of miles and hours away from me. But you know, that kind of distance and separation wasn't hard, because we understood the reason. Even as a small child I can remember weeping as I pictured the children, the hurting ones, the hungry ones my daddy was touching and helping. He made them real to us. He made that calling, that ministry, real to us.

"But you who have served Jesus know that there is an enemy who hates us, who is out to destroy us, who wants to hurt us any way he can, and who was angry at all the things that God had done through my father's life. He created a distance between my father and his family that couldn't be solved by getting on an airplane, a separation that was painful beyond words, which none of us wanted or even understood.

"There was a time, not long ago, when my father said to me, 'We'll be united in heaven, Honey. Our family will be together in heaven, all of us, perfectly. But I don't ever think it will happen here on earth.' At that time it had been nearly four years since we had been together as a family.

"But as you listen to what these wonderful men have said about my father, his ministry, and the work God did through him, I think you have to know that God wasn't going to let it end like that. You see, all aspects of life are important to God.

"And he was concerned with that little part of Daddy that belonged to us, too. And four days before Jesus took him home, my family was reunited.

"My father arranged for a beautiful hotel suite and called all of us and said, 'Come be with me.' Oh, it was a holy evening. It was a miracle of God. It was family. We laughed and joked and for the first time in over four years, my parents embraced. For us to see that, the reconciliation, the restoration, the victory over the vicious attempt of the enemy, was a miracle.

"I'm proud of my father. I said to my parents that evening, and I'll say to you and to them once again because I know Daddy's listening, 'Thank you for being our parents. More than that, thank you for being willing to be so wounded, to give so much for the kingdom of God.'

"You see, everybody gets hurt. Everybody suffers in this world. But so many people suffer for no reason, for nothing of lasting significance or consequence. I'm proud that what we gave was for this cause, that Jesus might be glorified. And I praise him for his faithfulness."

•　　•　　•

The Saturday following our evening together, Daddy videotaped a missionary endorsement. Recently, we all had the opportunity of viewing those few minutes of tape. We wept as we saw my father's familiar figure, slightly bent and a little frail, perhaps, but clothed in the power and authority of the one he served, proclaiming with a fire that only the Holy Spirit instills in the heart of a man the message of need and missionary challenge Satan had been unable to silence.

My single greatest concern is the growing inertia I see, inertia born out of our luxury and materialism. People are fooling themselves when they say the job is done. The vast body of people in the world today have never been given enough information to know if they accept or reject Jesus. Jesus commanded us to go to the uttermost parts of the earth. This has not been done yet in full. It cannot be said that all men or even half of all men have been reached for Jesus, despite all the tools and affluence we have to work with—more than any other people in history. . . . Most people think what the gospel needs is more clever, skilled people, when what it needs is more people who are willing to bleed, suffer, and die in a passion to see people come to Christ!

The small room was full of family and close friends, those who had known Daddy best and loved him most. As the screen went blank and the room fell silent, someone softly commented, *"That* was what the man was all about."

EPILOGUE

I was twenty-eight years old when I felt called to write *Man of Vision*. Today World Vision and I are well into our fifties and while World Vision has grown into the largest Christian relief and development organization in the world, God has continued to bless the little "brood" Daddy left behind. Bob and I will celebrate our thirtieth wedding anniversary in 2005. Our daughter, Michelle, has grown from a tender-hearted toddler into a beautiful woman of God. She and her husband, John, are both talented actors who have caught my father's vision to impact the world for Christ through television and film. Stacey, the baby Daddy blessed in my womb, is also married to a wonderful Christian man, and she and Vinnie have blessed us with two beautiful grandchildren. My sister, Robin, has three grown children . . . Christi, Jeffrey and Tony. And Sharon's daughter, Lisa, who already had one darling little girl, delighted us all by giving birth to triplets in 2001!

And then there is Mama. As I write this in June of 2004, Mother is still blessing us with her prayers and Godly encouragement. I am grateful that she has lived to see the incredible impact her life has had through both World Vision and Samaritan's Purse, now under

Franklin Graham's anointed leadership. But most of all I am grateful that she had the courage to share Daddy's and her personal story with the kind of transparent honesty that invites even the most broken of God's children to believe that God is bigger than any attack the enemy may devise against us. I suspect that this message of redemption and hope may be my parents' greatest legacy.

I remember the exact time and place when God put it on my heart to share the miracle of reconciliation that my family had experienced. I had never written anything of significance before and had no idea how God intended to use this modern-day epistle. Nor did I expect that twenty-five years later I would have reason to add a new ending chapter. But then God has a wonderful way of taking our simple acts of obedience and doing far beyond anything we could hope or imagine (Ephesians 3:20.)

In January of 2001—thirty-four years after my father resigned from World Vision—I joined the staff of World Vision US as a regional director with Women of Vision. Then in 2002 I was asked to become a national spokesperson for child sponsorship. To call this unexpected turn of events surprising is an understatement. Never in my wildest dreams did I expect that one day I would have the opportunity to see for myself the extreme poverty and suffering that God used to break my father's heart. Nor did I expect to have the joy of seeing how the seeds of ministry my father and mother planted so many years ago have flourished and grown. Today World Vision has an army of over twenty-two thousand dedicated staff bringing physical and spiritual transformation, compassion, and hope to desperately needy children and their communities in nearly a hundred countries around the world. What I have seen as I have traveled is nothing short of a miracle. And after all these years, child sponsorship is still at the heart of that miracle!

As I write this epilogue, over two million children and their families are being provided with nutritious food, clean water, healthcare, education, small business loans, and Christian witness. And by God's grace that number grows every year. I could go on and on, trying to describe the many ways sponsorship changes lives and give children a future and a hope. But, just as my father's letters have a way of taking us through time and space into the reality of his experience, I think the best way to describe the miracles I have seen is to take you with me on my second trip to Africa by way of my own personal journal. In January, 2002, I traveled to Sinazongwe, Zambia, to make a sponsorship video and meet one of the little girls my husband, Bob, and I sponsor . . . Oliviah.

January 8, 2002

Morning:

I met Oliviah today. My first impression was how small she is for ten. She isn't much taller than Vinnie (my six year old grandson.) My next thought was how solemn her expression was, but then life has not been kind to this stoic little girl. Oliviah's parents both died when she was two from AIDS.

Her village is located in a dusty, drought impacted area with only patches of green and a few barren trees. She lives in a small, two-room house built with clay bricks and sleeps with her two sisters on a mattress in a room the size of my closet. It is hot and musty. Yet Oliviah is blessed. She has a grandfather who obviously loves her, and two sister and four brothers who make her world rich with family. Her grandfather is also caring for nine other children left behind by the sons and daughters he has lost to AIDS . . . sixteen children in all!

I was told that Oliviah's day begins at 5, when she makes the first of several trips to the water well World Vision has provided for her village. Oliviah invited me to walk with her to draw water and I watched the tiny girl struggle to carry the five-gallon bucket back to her house. My first thought was that this was no job for a small child. But as I watched the fresh, clean water gush from the spout, I couldn't help thinking of the women I had met who walk miles every day in the hot sun to fill their containers with filthy, disease ridden water. And I realized that Oliviah and her village have been given a precious, life-giving gift in the simple, old-fashioned hand-pump . . . a gift made possible in part by the small check Bob and I write every month.

Then it was time to sit and get acquainted. We were immediately surrounded by at least thirty village children, all eager to see what I had brought. Oliviah was understandably shy, finding the cameras and attention being focused on her overwhelming. I did not see a real smile until I pulled out the stuffed cow I had brought her and made it "moo." As I had hoped, the cow made her laugh and I began to feel her relax. I continued to pull the small gifts I had brought out of my bag . . . coloring books, crayons, pencils, erasers. Every small offering produced excited murmurs from the crowd, as though I had produced treasures of great value.

While Oliviah examined her gifts, I asked her grandfather about the difference my sponsorship had made in Oliviah's life. He thought a moment, then explained that Oliviah had not been able to take her final exams last year to allow her to graduate from first to second grade. The reason was that he could not afford the paper exam book the school required. For want of a piece of paper, this bright little girl had not been allowed to continue her education! But now, because of our sponsorship, Oliviah has everything she needs for school and her grandfather was proud to report that she was doing very well!

Finally, I showed Oliviah pictures of my family. I explained that I had her picture on my refrigerator and that every day I prayed for her.

The words were no sooner out of my mouth than I realized that Oliviah had never seen a refrigerator and her blank look left me feeling a bit foolish. But I hoped she understood that I was trying to tell her that she was part of our family now and that we loved her.

Before we left, Oliviah and her sister offered to sing us a song. The girls giggled a bit as they worked up their courage, reminding me of my own little granddaughter when she performs for me in my living room. But when they finally began to sing, their clear, strong voices blew me away. I couldn't understand the words, but the obvious joy they felt had us all smiling and tapping our feet.

"What are they singing?" I asked our interpreter. "I call God on the telephone and he always answers," he replied with a grin.

I felt the tears come even as I had to laugh. What an amazing message from the heart of this little girl who had so little.

Two days later we came back to get a few pick-up shots and say goodbye. Two special moments will stay with me forever. When we arrived Oliviah ran into her house to get one of the coloring books I had brought her, so she could give me a picture as a keepsake. I followed her in, standing for a second to let my eyes adjust to the dim light. As I looked around, my eyes fell on a single picture frame hung upon the naked earthen wall. It was a collage of fading family pictures. I saw Oliviah's parents and grandparents and brothers and sisters. And there . . . right in the middle . . . was the picture of my family. Oliviah had us on her refrigerator!

The second happened as it came time to say our last goodbyes. I looked into the face of this little girl whom God had placed so uniquely in my family and in my heart, and I wondered what plans he had for her life. I found myself asking the age-old question we adults always ask the young. "What do you want to be when you grow up, Oliviah?"

I had asked the question many times before and thought I knew what her answer would be. Most children living in extreme poverty have dreams of becoming doctors or teachers or nurses, because these are the people who most positively impact their lives. But Oliviah didn't answer right away. Instead she looked down, seeming hesitant to speak. Then in a small voice she said, "I want to work for World Vision."

To this day my heart swells at the memory of that moment. I began my family's story with a question. "What does it take to touch the world for Christ . . . and when all is said and done, is it worth the price?" Now, as I picture Oliviah's earnest little face or imagine her drawing water from a gushing well or remember her singing praises to my Lord . . . and when I realize that everyday millions of children like Oliviah are being fed and clothed and educated and loved and given a future and a hope because of World Vision . . . I have my answer.